"The task of counseling is the task of loving others well. This book will help you to know what the love of Christ looks like, how to extend it to others, and how to accept it from others as you live in relationship together."

> **Heath Lambert,** Executive Director, Association of Certified Biblical Counselors; Associate Professor of Biblical Counseling, The Southern Baptist Theological Seminary; author, *The Biblical Counseling Movement after Adams*

"There are two things that Welch's book does very well. It demonstrates that no one gives grace better than a person who is convinced he needs it himself and that God makes his invisible grace visible by sending ordinary people to give extraordinary grace to people who need it. Welch not only reminds us all of our call to friendship ministry but also unpacks for us what it looks like. Every Christian should read this book!"

> **Paul David Tripp,** President, Paul Tripp Ministries; author, *What Did You Expect? Redeeming the Realities of Marriage*

"Welch builds a vision of a Christian community that moves beyond platitudes and empty promises to deep, scriptural, Christlike relationships. You will find this book to be a helpful primer on how to ask for and provide help in the midst of an age of separation."

> **Elyse M. Fitzpatrick,** counselor; speaker; author, *Found in Him*

"Finally! I've been wanting a book that helps normal, everyday Christians know how to help friends who are struggling. Ed Welch has given us this in his short, well-written, biblically sound, and Christ-exalting book. I'm planning to buy a bunch of copies and give it out to our church members."

> **Deepak Reju,** Pastor of Biblical Counseling and Family Ministry, Capitol Hill Baptist Church, Washington, DC; author, *The Pastor and Counseling*

"Ed Welch calls us back to the biblical model of one-another care with user-friendly wisdom that neither overcomplicates nor oversimplifies what it means to be a biblical encourager. I highly recommend *Side by Side* for every believer, every small group, and every church committed to being equipped to encourage one another in Christ."

> **Robert W. Kellemen,** Vice President, Institutional Development; Chair, Biblical Counseling Department, Crossroads Bible College; author, *Gospel-Centered Counseling*

"*Side by Side* is a simple, insightful, and practical guide to walking with people through times of trouble. This book will help churches to become communities of honesty and healing. You should read it—others will benefit, and so will you."

Ian Smith, Principal, Christ College, Sydney

"*Side by Side* is a very practical and thoroughly biblical guide meant as much for the average church member as for pastors and caregivers. Ed demolishes the myth that counseling can be done only by the professionally qualified. I wish this book had been written long ago."

John K. John, Executive Director, Biblical Counseling Trust of India

"This book of practical spirituality will produce many more helpless Christians, but also many more helpful Christians. It made me feel both more needy and more needed. A rare double blessing!"

David P. Murray, Professor of Old Testament and Practical Theology, Puritan Reformed Theological Seminary

"*Side by Side* is an expertly executed physical-therapy treatment for the disabled body of Christ. With biblical precision and practical compassion, Welch assists the attentive and teachable to work spiritual muscles left unused by many. Finally, someone has offered the people of God a ministry tool for mutual burden bearing and spiritual body building.

Joseph V. Novenson, Pastor, Lookout Mountain Presbyterian Church, Lookout Mountain, Tennessee

"Ed Welch skillfully provokes and counsels Christians on how to relate better with others by recognizing they are needy and needed. He puts his arms around church members who want to be more than spectators, around friends who want to grow in wise love for one another, and around parents who want to be more effective with their children. I wish I could have read this book as a young person—life would have been much richer both for others and for me."

Bruce K. Waltke, Professor Emeritus of Biblical Studies, Regent College

"*Side by Side* simply made my ministry approach and the necessary in-reach method more pertinent to successful personal outreach and up-close-and-personal discipleship."

Dallas H. Wilson Jr., Vicar, St. John's Chapel, Charleston, South Carolina

"We are needy people who share the same nature with many others in need of help. God's grace does not make us self-sufficient but enables us to help others. Welch develops this principle beautifully in this book. *Side by Side* is not only a book for individual profit but one to be used as an instrument for the growth of the church and the equipping of God's people."

Valdeci Santos, Vice-President and Professor of Biblical Counseling and Missions, Andrew Jumper Graduate Center, Brazil

"*Side by Side* is a practical book about us needing others and others needing us. It pushes us to go further in our relationships and offers concrete ways to do that. It is a book about being companions and allies in Christian living. It is a book, finally, about being good Christian friends. I'd love every member of our church to read it—we would be a stronger community as a result."

Steve Midgley, Executive Director, Biblical Counselling UK; Senior Minister, Christ Church, Cambridge

Side by Side

Walking with Others in Wisdom and Love

Edward T. Welch

CROSSWAY®

WHEATON, ILLINOIS

Side by Side: Walking with Others in Wisdom and Love

Copyright © 2015 by Edward T. Welch

Published by Crossway
        1300 Crescent Street
        Wheaton, Illinois 60187

Cover design: Faceout Studio

First printing 2015

Printed in the United States of America

Unless otherwise indicated, Scripture quotations are from the ESV® Bible (The Holy Bible, English Standard Version®), copyright © 2001 by Crossway. Used by permission. All rights reserved.

Scripture references marked NIV are taken from *The Holy Bible, New International Version*®, NIV®. Copyright © 1973, 1978, 1984, 2011 by Biblica, Inc.™ Used by permission. All rights reserved worldwide.

Trade paperback ISBN: 978-1-4335-4711-9
ePub ISBN: 978-1-4335-4714-0
PDF ISBN: 978-1-4335-4712-6
Mobipocket ISBN: 978-1-4335-4713-3

Library of Congress Cataloging-in-Publication Data

Welch, Edward T., 1953–
   Side by side : walking with others in wisdom and love /
Edward T. Welch.
      pages cm
   Includes bibliographical references and index.
   ISBN 978-1-4335-4711-9 (tp)
   1. Helping behavior—Religious aspects—Christianity.
2. Caring—Religious aspects—Christianity. 3. Friendship—
Religious aspects—Christianity. I. Title.
BV4647.H4W45   2015
241'.4—dc23   2014026789

Crossway is a publishing ministry of Good News Publishers.

RRD		25	24	23	22	21	20	19	18	17	16
16	15	14	13	12	11	10	9	8	7	6	5	4

To
Sharon

Contents

Introduction

Side by Side: Needy and Needed

This book identifies the skills we need to help one another.

It is for everyone—friends, parents, even neighbors.

Along the way we will find that God is pleased to use ordinary people, ordinary conversations, and extraordinary and wise love to do most of the heavy lifting in his kingdom.

The basic idea is that those who help best are the ones who both need help and give help. A healthy community is dependent on all of us being both. So the book is divided into two parts. The first part guides you in sharing your burdens; the second part guides you in bearing the burdens of others.

We all need help—that's simply part of being human.

The help we need goes beyond things like getting our house painted or finding a good mechanic. It's deeper than that. We need help for our *souls*, especially when we are going through hardships. Help can be as simple as connecting with someone who understands or with someone who genuinely says, "I'm so sorry." We were not designed to go through hard things alone.

But it's not easy to ask for help. We spend a lot of time hiding our neediness because we are afraid of what people will think. Speaking personally, on most days I am happy to give help and reluctant to ask for it. For me, being needy is a sign of weakness, and, given a choice, I prefer to appear strong or at least competent.

Yet weakness—or neediness—is a valuable asset in God's community. Jesus introduced a new era in which weakness is the new strength. Anything that reminds us that we are dependent on God and other people is a good thing. Otherwise, we trick ourselves into thinking that we are self-sufficient, and arrogance is sure to follow. We need help, and God has given us his Spirit and each other to provide it.

We are all helpers—this too is part of being human. A young child is most satisfied when helping parents cook or clean. They delight in contributing to the household. In this, they illustrate how God has given all people gifts "for the common good" (1 Cor. 12:7), and all gifts are needed. There is no such thing as an unnecessary person.

Actually, we offer help so often that we might not even be aware of it. We listen to a roommate or a spouse about struggles at work, we commiserate with a friend who is full of fears, we give advice to the member of our small group who is going through a bumpy relationship, we ask how we can pray.

We were meant to live that way. We were meant to walk side by side, an interdependent body of weak people. God is pleased to grow and change us through the help of people who have been re-created in Christ and empowered by the Spirit. That is how life in the church works.

And yet fear enters in. We are afraid to jump into the complexities of someone's life. Who are we to help someone else? We have troubles galore. Our past makes a mess of the present. Sin always threatens to overtake us. And who doesn't have a psychological disorder? We feel broken ourselves and fear we will only make things worse for others. We feel unqualified.

In our era we consult experts, professionals, and specialists, but when you look at your own history of having been helped, it's likely that you'll notice very few experts among those who have helped you. Who were your helpers? Were they professional counselors or specialists? Probably not. Most often, they were friends—the regular, everyday people in your life. Friends are the best helpers. They come prepackaged with compassion and love. All they need is wisdom, and that is available to everyone.

It's the perfect system. If God used only experts and people of renown, some could boast in their own wisdom, but God's way of doing things is not the same as our way. We ordinary people have been given power and wisdom through the Holy Spirit and are called to love others (John 13:34). From this beginning, we are compelled to move toward others rather than stay away.

So I am writing for people like me, who are willing to move toward other struggling people but are not confident that they can say or do anything very helpful. If you feel quite weak and ordinary—if you feel like a mess but have the Spirit—you have the right credentials. You are one of the ordinary people God uses to help others.

As we get the knack of this rhythm—being needy and needed—Jesus will be in it and over it. He was weak before we were; he was dependent on his Father and dependent even on mere human beings. He also came to serve rather than to be served, and he did it side by side. As far as we are able, we do this with one another.

Part 1

We Are Needy

Your neediness qualifies you to help others. Your neediness, offered well to someone else, can even be one of the great gifts you give to your church. You will inspire others to ask for help.

Think of a time when you were in a group and someone spoke openly about a struggle in daily life. What happened next? In most instances, the group suddenly became more like a family. Other people opened up about their lives, and the prayers of the group sounded more and more like the Psalms. When something like this happens, the myth that we all have life figured out is exposed, and we begin to share one another's burdens, which is the way God intended it to be.

We spend too much time concealing our neediness. We need to stop hiding. Being needy is our basic condition. There is no shame in it—it's just the way it is. Understanding this, accepting it, and practicing it will make you a better helper.

This part of the book begins with a simple sketch of who we are. From there, it will help you understand, admit, and practice your own neediness.

We Are Needy

Life Is Hard

Our Hearts Are Busy

Hard Circumstances Meet Busy Hearts

Sin Weighs a Lot

Say "Help" to the Lord

Say "Help" to Other People

1

Life Is Hard

Life is too hard to manage single-handedly. That's why we are
needy. Life is also good, but it is hard. There is never a day when
we have immunity from difficult circumstances.

To admit that is not complaining. It is simply true. Jesus
said, "In the world you will have tribulation" (John 16:33), and,
if we stop to think about those tribulations, we realize they are
unending:

- Our health
- Job and financial unknowns
- Local violence
- Broken promises
- Too much to do
- Our family's health
- Discrimination and injustice
- International terrorism
- Conflict with friends
- Mechanical breakdowns

Why do we bother identifying such hardships? We do it because human beings do best when they take their hardships
public to God and at least one other person. When we survey
the Psalms, we discover that this is God's desire for us.

> To you, O Lord, I cry,
> and to the Lord I plead for mercy. (Ps. 30:8)

Through psalms like that one, the Lord essentially says to us, "Come to me with your hardships. That's what children do with their Father." The hard things of life are important to God, and if they are important to God, they are important to us, and we will labor to put them into speech.

Life Organized

Where do we start? Since there is so much, it might help to organize the circumstances of our lives. Figure 1, below, is a way to do that. It organizes those circumstances, both good and hard, in a series of concentric circles. Think of it as an X-ray of ourselves and the world around us. The heart and the first circle (our body) represent us; the additional concentric circles are circumstances that surround us. They are the world in which we live.

Figure 1. A biblical X-ray of a person and the surrounding world

Consider first a few of those circumstances that shape our lives. (We will deal with the heart in the next chapter.)

Our Body

Our body is an integral part of us, but it is also a kind of circumstance that affects us. It blesses us with health, and it brings hardships such as daily aches and pains, sleep loss, headaches, and the gamut of medical diagnoses. The body, including the brain, contributes to psychiatric diagnoses. If you're experiencing mania, certain features of depression, or attention deficits—the list can be long—there might be elusive yet physical problems coming at you.

Our Relationships

Relationships are where we find the best and worst of life. Here is the pleasure of growing and peaceful relationships, and here is where hopes are dashed and love is lost. Here is where we experience aloneness, victimization, and rejection. Whether or not we like it, we need people, but they can make life difficult.

Our Work

Work includes the job we have or would like to have, the futility of some work, and the money we earn. Money, in particular, can have a significant influence on our lives. Both poverty and riches leave us vulnerable. Poverty suggests that God is not with us, so we trust in ourselves, and riches suggest that we have what we need, so we trust in our money. Work and money shape our lives more than we know.

Spiritual Beings and the World

Spiritual beings are behind the scenes, but they pack a punch. Angels protect us, while spiritual beings in cahoots with Satan oppose us. These spiritual beings have power to afflict us physically, as we see with Job. But their primary weapons are lies, half-truths, and temptations, tactics that are much more powerful than any physical affliction.

The world is included among these influences. Scripture uses *world* in two different ways. Sometimes *world* means the inhabited creation, in other words, the earth. Other times, and the way I am using it here, it refers to Satan and those who stand hand in hand with his against-God ways. Together they create a chorus of voices that quietly yet powerfully speak against the character of God and announce that sin is just fine. You can hear the world especially in our culture's chorus about sexual license. This means that we are, indeed, vulnerable people who need God's power and protection (e.g., Eph. 6:10–12).

The Triune God and His Kingdom

The circle that envelops everything is God himself. We live, in all ways and at all times, before God—Father, Son, and Spirit—and in his world (Acts 17:28). God is over all things and surrounds all our circumstances. He is sovereign and active, never asleep. God is in the details of daily life; he is in the broad strokes of history as he moves all things to a final climax, and we need him in order to "have life and have it abundantly" (John 10:10). He is by no means a bystander, off on the side, silently observing our troubles—though we could easily think such things. Instead, he created all things, so he owns all things.

We could add more circles. Ethnic and religious heritage is *the* circumstance of life for many people. We could also add our geographical and political environment, but those listed above can get us started. Life includes so many influences and hardships, and God is up to something in all of them.

Think about what you would jot down in those circles. What comes to mind? What is good, and, especially, what is hard?

Our task for now is to acknowledge some specifics of the fragility and uncertainty of our lives and the difficult circumstances we face and then to speak about them to God. Just speak. That is his desire—for us to speak honestly from our heart. We don't have to add requests. Just speak.

Discussion and Response

1) There are a lot of hard things coming at you. What are the top three? You could also take one from each of the categories that surround each one of us.

2) Take time to speak your hard things to the Lord-who-hears.

We Are Needy

Life Is Hard

Our Hearts Are Busy

Hard Circumstances Meet Busy Hearts

Sin Weighs a Lot

Say "Help" to the Lord

Say "Help" to Other People

2

Our Hearts Are Busy

The circumstances of life are easy to understand, but it is at the center of these—our hearts—where things get complicated. Our hearts are always stirring with activity. They guide our thoughts and actions as we interact with all our circumstances: our body, our relationships, our work, spiritual beings and the world, and God. Here in the heart we find the very essence of who we are. Our hearts are seen most readily through our emotions but are also expressed in the good—and the bad—that we do. And our connection to God resides here. Yes, our hearts are busy.

Since Scripture itself is so interested in our hearts, it uses a rich and varied vocabulary to identify this controlling center of life. *Spirit, soul, heart, mind, inner person,* and *conscience* are the most familiar terms. Each of those words has a particular emphasis, but they have one thing in common. They all identify our *spiritual* center, that is, how we are connected to God, at all times, whether we know it or not.

It is tough to picture something you cannot see, and you cannot see the actual heart, but Scripture does provide images and analogies such as a fountainhead, a well, a tree, and a treasure chest.[1]

A fountainhead is the real source of the more visible streams (Prov. 4:23), and a well has depths that must be drawn out (Prov. 20:5). They can yield either fetid water or living water (John 7:38).

A tree has roots that search for a life source (Jer. 17:5–8). Either those roots will find their rest in other people, which Scripture likens to being a withering shrub in the desert, or they will settle for nothing but the Lord alone, in which case they will be sustained through the most difficult times.

A treasure chest is where we put our valuables (Matt. 6:19–21). This is what we truly love. Some treasure is prone to rust and corruption—we can be sure that our fears would accompany such a treasure. Other treasure is stored away in Jesus and is secure.

These pictures capture how our hearts work behind the scenes, quietly determining the course of our lives, and have much more to do with God than we might realize.They can also be brought into the light and examined. One way to do that is by following our emotions.

Emotions Come from the Heart

Our emotions are our first response to the world around us. They appear without any apparent thought. Yet they are much more than mere reactions in that they say more about *us* than they do about our circumstances. Our emotions, it turns out, reveal what is most dear to us (e.g., Pss. 25:17; 45:1). That's why our emotions identify us. They *are* us. We recognize our friends by their passions and emotional responses. When our friends' emotions are blunted by head injury or intensified by side effects of medication, we say that they are not themselves. Our emotions point out those things that are most important to us.

When happy, we possess something we love; when anxious, something we love is at risk; when despondent, something we love has been lost; when angry, something we love is being stolen or kept from us.

Or look at guilt and shame. We might not say that they reveal what we love, but they certainly reveal what is dear to us. When we feel shame, we feel as though someone has taken off our human covering and left us naked. It separates us from relationships, and relationships are dear to us. When guilty, we feel like our relationship with *God* is potentially in jeopardy, and this relationship gets to matters of life and death.

What is most important to us? What do we love? What is most dear to us?[2] We shouldn't be surprised that these questions get to the core of our being. They also point to where we are headed. All roads eventually lead to our relationship with God. Do we love what he loves? Is *he* most dear to us?

So track down those strong feelings, first in yourself and then in others. When do you notice yourself getting excited? What are your joys? Your sorrows? Watch friends light up when they talk about a child, a spouse, a musical group, Jesus, work, or a sport. We will hear them slow down when touching on something that is especially hard, as if they were suddenly carrying a weight. We might notice a flash of anger: "I will *never* be like my father." If we are trusted, we might hear of fears, hidden pain, and shame—matters that we prefer to keep private.

We could sum up our emotions this way: they usually proceed from our hearts, are given shape by our bodies, reflect the quality of our relationships, bear the etchings of both the goodness and the meaninglessness of work, provide a peek into how we fare in spiritual battle, and identify what we really believe about God.

One qualification: we could say that emotions *usually* reflect what is happening in our hearts. Occasionally, since emotions are given shape by our bodies, emotions can be unpredictable assaults that come from disordered bodies and unruly brains.

Depression, for example, might say that something loved is now lost, life has lost meaning and purpose, or something desired will never be possessed. But depression could also say, "Something is not right in my body or brain."

In other words, strong emotions are a time to ask, "What is my heart really saying? What do I live for that I do not have?" But we might not get clear answers to those questions. Sometimes depression is simply physical suffering. It says, "I feel as though I am numb inside." Either way—and this is important—difficult emotions are always a time to get help and pray for endurance in faith. A depressed person is suffering, and suffering leaves us spiritually vulnerable. It raises questions about God's goodness and care, and it whispers that we must have done something bad to deserve such suffering. Emotional suffering needs spiritual encouragement.

Good Comes from the Heart

Now let's go a little deeper. Our emotions can be right on the surface and obvious to us. But farther in is everything we would call "good."

This good, like our emotions, still expresses what we love and desire. But it points even more obviously to God. For example, parents love their children. That love, whether or not parents know it, reflects the love of God for his children, and it is good. There is good in every human being. Even the blatant narcissist has a softer, good side if we look closely enough. Since God created us, and created things always bear some quality of their creator, we are able to see good things in one another. It comes in so many forms:

- Neighbors help each other.
- Strangers return lost wallets.
- Employees work hard, even when the boss is on vacation.
- Spouses acknowledge when they are wrong.
- Car mechanics are honest.

When goodness is our response to Jesus—when we do good because of him—it can also be called "obedience," "faith," or an "expression of our love for God." This goodness is especially beautiful when hardships seem to rain on us, and, in response, we turn to the Lord rather than away from him. The good shines brightest in weakness. This is the essence of faith, and it compels our admiration. Anything we do because of Jesus—love, work, endure, hope—is *very* good.

Our eye for God's reflected goodness is important in the way we help, and we will come back to it over and over. Help includes seeing what is good in another person.

Bad Comes from the Heart

All, of course, is not well. Our hearts can be good, but they can also be very bad. They are both at the same time.

Although we prefer to keep this reality under wraps, there is little disagreement about the badness resident in every heart. We all know that we do wrong. We love ourselves more than we love others. Selfishness and pride are part of everyday life:

- Parents demean and tear down their children.
- Neighbors gossip.
- Employees defraud employers.
- Men love pornography more than they love their spouses.
- Contractors charge for unnecessary work.

Yet while we all acknowledge the bad within us, we are less willing to acknowledge that it is sin. *Sin* means that our badness is primarily directed against God, and most people are not consciously shaking their fist at God. Instead, we are not thinking about him at all. So how can bad behavior be sin?

This is where things get murky, and we need the light that Scripture brings. Though we live before God, we are not always *conscious* of God. When a teen violates a parent's directions, it doesn't always feel like an act of rebellion against the parent. It typically feels simpler—the teen just wants to do what he or she wants to do. The disobedience is "nothing personal," but it *is* personal. The same is true for us. When we sin, it is against God, even if it doesn't feel that way.

Then there is more conscious bad behavior. A man had to choose between cocaine and his wife: "It was clear to me that there wasn't a choice. I love my wife, but I'm not going to choose *anything* over cocaine."[3]

There is the heart in action. That man loves his desires above his wife. That's clear. You know it, he knows it, and it is bad. Now peer just a little further in and you discover that he loves his desires above the Lord—he is committed to manage his life his way rather than submit to the Lord. He won't be conscious of that, but he might acknowledge it when he hears it.

We are, indeed, needy people.

Figure 2.

Spiritual Allegiances Come from the Heart

At the very center of our hearts is our connection to God. Here are the roots of the tree, the spring at the bottom of the well. Whether or not we know it, we are religious through and through.

We could call it "worship"—that's what is happening in our hearts. Who we love above all else is who we worship, and who we worship controls us.

Whether or not we realize it, our hearts know a lot about the true God, and we take our stand for or against him. That knowledge is not always obvious to us, but it is there. It is as if we retain some vague awareness of the love songs that God sang to us before we went our own way, and when we hear them again, they evoke something familiar and right. He is our Father; we are his children. We live *coram Deo*, before the face of God. There is no such thing as independence. Even if we run away, he is our Father. Even if we apply for legal emancipation, we cannot escape. Here are just a few ways we know this:

- Our hearts recognize his voice. We know love because he is love. We want justice because he is the righteous judge. We are drawn to compassion and mercy because he is the compassionate and merciful God (Ex. 34:6).

- Our hearts have the "work of the law" written on them (Rom. 2:15), and that law reflects God's character. We have a conscience that condemns the wrong and approves of the right.

- Our hearts are never fully at rest until we rest in him.

- Our hearts are at their best when we love and worship the triune God above all else and follow his commands.

What confuses matters is that the sins of others, the lies of the Evil One, and our own sins can distort this knowledge.

Fearful people know God, but they see first the masks of those who have hurt them.

Those who feel guilty might assume that God is like a mere human being who forgives begrudgingly and with strings attached.

Those who hate others have pushed aside the truth that God extends his love even to enemies.

Those who always want more from life know God but believe the lie that there is satisfaction outside of God.

Mingled with the knowledge of the true God are lies we bring and lies we are told. The result is that no one has a completely unhindered and accurate knowledge of the Lord. No one. Our resident myths are revealed in our fears, pasts, troubled emotions, and sins.

Given this picture of humanity, an accurate knowledge of God is the most important thing—the most healthy and joy-producing thing—we could have. And it is exactly what our Father delights to give us.

Notice how the apostle Paul prays for us:

> I do not cease to give thanks for you, remembering you in my prayers, that the God of our Lord Jesus Christ, the Father of glory, may give you the Spirit of wisdom and of revelation in the knowledge of him. (Eph. 1:16–17; see also 3:14–19)

Paul understands that the deepest need of our hearts is God—to know him accurately and follow him. This means that if we want to both be helped and truly help others, we will always be aiming for this. And since Jesus himself is our fullest picture of God, we will always be aiming for him. Somehow, as we grow in our knowledge and worship of Jesus, he encourages the good, rehabilitates the bad, and brings peace to a troubled heart. He is the source of all wisdom, love, and hope. Whether or not we say the actual name of Jesus to a needy friend, we always aim for Jesus.

Then, with a growing knowledge of Jesus in hand, we respond by believing and following him.

The heart is busy. It is our spiritual center. The evidence for its activity can be seen every day in the human mash-up of good, bad, fears, frustrations, joys, and sorrows. Trace these to the heart's very core and we come face-to-face with the true God and the condition of our relationship to him. Are we trying to eke out an existence by ourselves in the desert, or are we busily sending out roots by the water?

Discussion and Response

1) Can you describe the heart in a few sentences?
2) Give some examples of how your feelings are linked to what is happening in your relationship with God.

We Are Needy

Life Is Hard

Our Hearts Are Busy

Hard Circumstances Meet Busy Hearts

Sin Weighs a Lot

Say "Help" to the Lord

Say "Help" to Other People

3

Hard Circumstances Meet Busy Hearts

Troubling circumstances will always come. Life *is* hard. When difficult circumstances and our hearts meet, a conversation breaks out between the two—back and forth, back and forth—and the conversation can be wise and hopeful, or it can be foolishness that parades as wisdom.

The Conversation Begins

Our troubles usually start the internal conversation:

> "This is painful. Why is this happening?"

Then it gets messy. Spiritual beings whisper, "Does God really care? Can his words be trusted?" Our hearts can submit to those questions, and we can adopt them as our own:

> "Maybe he doesn't really care. Wouldn't a good father protect his children from these things?"

Meanwhile God himself speaks.

We could condense his many words this way: "Look to Jesus, crucified and raised from the dead. The crucified one who suffered—he is the evidence of unfailing love in affliction. Suffering raises many questions, and for most of those questions you will have to trust me—that my love is more sophisticated than you know."

Our task is to hear God's voice, believe his words, and follow Jesus even when life is hard.

Back and forth, back and forth. Trouble comes at us; we respond. The Devil questions our responses; we respond. God's Word in Jesus Christ tells the real story about our suffering and speaks hope; we respond. And the conversation continues.

Who wins? Who will have the final word?

Meanwhile, the conversation actually changes the experience of suffering. For example, if we respond with, "Everything is meaningless, and God does not care," our pain will be worse. If we respond with, "I don't understand all this, but I know that my Father loves me, and I trust him," we will live with purpose, hope, and perseverance. If we remember the promises of God in our testing and turn to him, trouble can feel light and momentary (2 Cor. 4:17) when compared to the riches we have in him.

It is in this back and forth that we need help. Even those who seem strong in their faith can be left wobbly by sufferings that threaten the things they love most.

Some Conversations Go Better than Others

There are some conversations in which the heart does not want help. We have had enough and are adamant, and no words from God or other people will sway us. Here is one of those:

"God, you have no heart." He was a quiet God-fearer. Some would call him shy. Neighbors rarely heard him speak, though they would say he was a good neighbor.

When he was removed from his home and relocated to a Hungarian ghetto, he was the same old person, as if nothing had changed. But when he was herded into a truck that was far too small for the dozens of people onboard, when the trip was in its second and then third day without water, when guards opened the doors every few hours and randomly rammed the butts of their rifles onto infirmed heads, and when people were dying around him, his heart finally responded.

His circumstances dominated the inner free-for-all.

"Almighty God, why have you done this to us? Have you no heart, no feelings? Have you no eyes to see with? Have you no ears to hear us with? You are wicked, O Lord, as wicked as a man."[4]

That was the end of his conversation. He indicted God and felt that there was nothing more to say. Rather than borrow the words from the psalms of David, he responded with his own anti-psalm, and he was sticking with it.

Here is a better conversation:

"Nothing has changed." A fifty-four-year-old father of four had a long history of walking with Jesus. One of his routines was to read a psalm every day, and Psalm 22 was one of his favorites. Since he had done this for decades, he certainly was accustomed to speaking honestly to the Lord in all circumstances, and he, too, could condense his reactions into a few words.

During a routine exam, his physician noticed a highly irregular lesion on his shoulder, which he biopsied and sent to a pathology lab for testing. The results would be back in about ten days. The physician was clearly concerned and suggested that his patient return to the office to discuss the results and consider whatever further treatments might be helpful.

Ten days later, he made the visit, accompanied by his wife. The doctor got right to the point.

"I have bad news. The lesion is cancerous."

"What does that mean? What is the treatment and prognosis?"

"It is a malignant melanoma—one of the most aggressive cancers. At this point, the only treatments we have are experimental, and they have not shown much promise."

"And the prognosis?"

"I am very sorry. Life expectancy is usually between nine and twelve months."

He thanked the physician for being helpful, clear, and forthright. They arranged a follow-up appointment to talk about experimental treatments. He and his wife left the office and cried together.

His first words were, "Nothing has changed."

In the face of the worst possible circumstance for both himself and his family, he said, "Nothing has changed." His heart and its clear-eyed knowledge of Jesus hijacked the internal conversation and essentially said this: "If you think that news of my death will change my confidence in God's love toward me, it won't. His Son gave his life for me. Why would I think he would love me less now? He loved me yesterday when everything seemed to be going well. Nothing has changed—he loves me today too."

That was the final word. There was so much to do, and many tears would follow. Indeed, he asked for prayer from family and friends—for faith, for hope, for love—but he never revised that initial conversation, even though he died, surrounded by his family, a year later.

Here is the best one: *"Why have you forsaken me?"* Jesus has gone before us and shows us how to respond to hardships—how to have the heart conversation with God. This is how Jesus responded to his suffering:

My God, my God, why have you forsaken me?
  Why are you so far from saving me, from the words of
    my groaning?
O my God, I cry by day, but you do not answer,
  and by night, but I find no rest. (Ps. 22:1–2)

Honest, open cries spoken to the Father—that was his way of responding to hardships. He begins with questions. Why is this happening? How could this be? Why are you so far away? Why don't you answer?

Jesus's words seem shocking in their desperation, yet he authorizes the use of these very words in our own troubles. What is especially important, however, is that he is not grumbling or challenging God with his words. No, he is crying out and directing his words *to* the promise-making and promise-keeping God, who really does hear. Doing this is much harder than it looks, given our tendency to turn inward in our pain.

Since it makes no sense that his Father would be silent and distant, he continues:

Yet you are holy,
  enthroned on the praises of Israel.
In you our fathers trusted;
  they trusted, and you delivered them.
To you they cried and were rescued;
  in you they trusted and were not put to shame.
    (vv. 3–5)

His cry to the Father goes in many directions. He praises the Father and speaks of desperate times in Israel's past when God rescued and delivered them. Jesus does spiritual battle by always bringing the conversation back to his Father's reliable and proven words and deeds. There is no chaos here—the voice of the Father has clear authority over all others.

> Yet you are he who took me from the womb;
>> you made me trust you at my mother's breasts.
> On you was I cast from my birth,
>> and from my mother's womb you have been my God.
>> (vv. 9–10)

So in the midst of his dire circumstances, he calls out to the one who hears and acts:

> But you, O LORD, do not be far off!
>> O you my help, come quickly to my aid! . . .
>> Save me from the mouth of the lion! (vv. 19–21)

And the conversation continues. He moves effortlessly from pleas for help to declarations of deliverance. These declarations reach their zenith when Jesus brings past, present, and future together, even from the cross, and finishes his plea with these words: "You have rescued me" (v. 21).

From there Jesus goes public with his praise and considers the certainties of the future:

> I will tell of your name to my brothers;
>> in the midst of the congregation I will praise you:
> You who fear the LORD, praise him!
>> All you offspring of Jacob, glorify him,
>> and stand in awe of him, all you offspring of Israel!
> For he has not despised or abhorred
>> the affliction of the afflicted,
> and he has not hidden his face from him,
>> but has heard, when he cried to him. (vv. 22–24)

The Father, Jesus says, has not hidden his face. The Father has heard his cries. Then Jesus reminds us to turn to the Lord, for he has done good to us:

All the ends of the earth shall remember
    and turn to the LORD,
and all the families of the nations
    shall worship before you. . . .
Posterity shall serve him;
    it shall be told of the Lord to the coming generation;
they shall come and proclaim his righteousness to a people
      yet unborn,
    that he has done it. (vv. 27–31)

That is one of many psalms that will help us learn how to direct our inner conversations with God when trouble comes. There are an endless number of ways to conduct this dialogue. Psalm 22, however, deserves special attention because it was Jesus's most anguished cry. As such, it can be a template for our own misery, no matter how extreme.

Keep Talking, Grow during Trouble

So we keep talking to God, not grumbling about him. Most of us fall between the two extremes of Psalm 22 and the anti-psalm of the man facing Nazi oppression. Most of us have our moments when suffering has the power to turn our hearts hard. For some, that place is even as simple as a flat tire or some mechanical mishap, especially if it's one of many. For others the line is not crossed until the life of a loved one is in jeopardy. Yet for people like the apostle Paul and the man who said, "Nothing has changed," there is no line. No amount of suffering can shake their confidence in God. I fear that my own line is closer to the flat tire.

With God's help, we grow. We aspire to make the psalms more and more our own. When trouble comes and the free-for-all breaks out, we will be able to restore order. If order doesn't come, we get more help. We aim to create our own psalms in which we (1) pour out our complaint to the Lord, (2) review God's promises and his faithfulness, (3) find our rest and comfort in Jesus, and (4) let others know that they, too, can find rest and comfort. Then, when we falter, we ask for help and do it all again.

One of the critical spiritual skills for every follower of Jesus is to bring order to the internal ruckus and *grow* in trouble rather than rage or wither in it (2 Cor. 4:16). Tribulation will not win in the end. In the midst of physical misery we can have hope, and hope is one of our most valued responses to the difficulties of life.

Discussion and Response

1) Take a recent difficult event and identify what kind of psalm you are writing.
2) Paraphrase Psalm 22 and let the psalmist guide you in prayer.

We Are Needy

Life Is Hard

Our Hearts Are Busy

Hard Circumstances Meet Busy Hearts

Sin Weighs a Lot

Say "Help" to the Lord

Say "Help" to Other People

4

Sin Weighs a Lot

Suffering *feels* like our biggest problem and avoiding it like our greatest need—but we know that there is something more. Sin is actually our biggest problem, and rescue from it is our greatest need.

There is a link between the two. Suffering exposes the sin in our hearts in a way that few things can. When our lives are trouble free, we can confuse personal satisfaction for faith. We can think that God is good, and we are pleased with him, though we might be pleased less with him than we are with the ease of our lives. Then, when life is hard—especially when life *remains* hard—the allegiances of our hearts become more apparent. Suffering will reveal sin that still "clings so closely" to us (Heb. 12:1), and sin weighs a lot.

We don't always like to look at it, but this burden needs to be dealt with. Sin is the heaviest of weights; forgiveness is the greatest deliverance.

See the Weight

Only people who know they have burdens can be delivered from them. Sadly, the method for that deliverance—confession—has been tarnished. We are slow to talk about sin for fear that it could threaten our already fragile egos or label us as judgmental and narrow-minded. But instead of thinking about sin talk as an endless stream of negativity and browbeating, think of it as something good. It is, after all, a part of God's rescue package that is called the "Good News."

So though it's true that sin itself is not good, to see our sin *is* good. Whereas sin leads down a burden-filled path, Jesus says, "I came that they may have life and have it abundantly" (John 10:10). Confession is essential to that life.

Seeing the weight of our sin brings blessings. Here are three:

1) Seeing the weight of our sin drives us to Jesus.

It is the Spirit's work to help us see our sin (John 16:8). This drives us to Jesus for forgiveness, and this is very good. Jesus comes for sinners, not the righteous (Matt. 9:13). Conviction of sin shows that we are alive and responsive. Conviction means that we can see ourselves, at least partly, and that is a prerequisite for talking with friends about sins (Matt. 7:3–5).

With no need for mercy, why bother sticking with Jesus? If we look to him merely for deliverance from life's difficult circumstances, we would do better with Prozac or a little cunning. These, at least in the short term, seem more effective.

2) Seeing the weight of our sin brings humility.

An awareness of sin brings humility—not shame or humiliation—and humility is a brilliant reflection of Jesus to others.

> The tax collector, standing far off, would not even lift up his eyes to heaven, but beat his breast, saying, "God, be merciful to me, a sinner!" I tell you, this man went down to his house justified, rather than the other. For everyone who

exalts himself will be humbled, but the one who humbles himself will be exalted. (Luke 18:13–14)

Here is a community goal: to be able to identify one pattern of sin in our lives, and to be able to do it with only a moment's notice any time we are asked.

3) Seeing the weight of our sin is the beginning of power and confidence.

When we see our sin, we are seeing the Spirit's conviction, which means we are witnessing spiritual power, but that power feels different from what we expect. It's not like worldly power. Spiritual power feels like a struggle, or weakness, or neediness, or desperation. It is simply, "I need Jesus," which is the most powerful thing we can say. It means that our confidence is not in ourselves or in either our righteousness before God or our reputation before others. Our confidence is in Jesus, and that confidence cannot be shaken. Just imagine: no more hiding from God, no more defensiveness in our relationships. When we have wronged others, we simply ask their forgiveness. Our security in Jesus gives us the opportunity to think less often about what others think of us. It gives us freedom to make mistakes and even fail. No longer do we have to build and protect our own kingdom.

Sins weighs a lot, but those who can see their sins see something good. When we confess these sins, knowing that they are forgiven, we see something better—Jesus himself.

Lay the Weight Down

So we want to grow in seeing sin and confessing it. We want to lay the weight down. But it's not always easy. Young children confess blatant disobedience—"I'm sorry I threw my dolly at you"—but the ins and outs of that disobedience are lost on them. We, too, can be children. Consider the man caught in pornography whose confession—"I'm sorry, okay?"—doesn't measure up to a child's. Such confessions, from an adult, are unbecoming and hurtful. To lay the weight of sin down means looking more carefully at our hearts.

"Against you, you only, have I sinned" (Ps. 51:4).

Though we don't always realize it, all sin is personal—it is against God. It is against God and his character. Our sin says, "I want my independence"; "I don't want to be associated with you"; "I want more than you can offer me"; "I know what is best for me"; or—and this is scary—"I hate you" (James 4:4). We don't always know we are saying these things, but that is the nature of the heart. There is usually more going on than what we see.

Throughout biblical history, God has graciously let his people see the realities of their hearts. When he liberated his people from Egypt and led them into the desert on the way to a fruitful land, the people grumbled against Moses and Aaron, wondering, as many of us would, why they were being taken out of Egypt only to face other hardships in the desert.

Moses saw clearly: "Your grumbling is not against us but against the LORD" (Ex. 16:8). No one had said a word against God, but in reality they all had. The Lord himself responded to Moses by exposing the truth:

> The LORD said to Moses, "How long will this people despise me? And how long will they not believe in me, in spite of all the signs that I have done among them?" (Num. 14:11)

And all they did was a little grumbling during a challenging day.

The New Testament letter from James follows up on this insight (James 4:1–10). James takes us from things that are obvious, such as disputes and quarrels, and then moves to things that are less obvious, such as our out-of-control desires and demands, our unfaithfulness to God, our friendship with both the world and the Devil, and our hatred against God. What has seemed like a perfectly good reason to get ticked off at someone becomes a time for the Spirit to take us into depths we could not see without him.

Let's keep that understanding of our hearts in mind. Bad behaviors, even those that are culturally acceptable, like a little grumbling, are expressions of our spiritual allegiances. And through confession we invite God's spotlight on those uneven and divided allegiances.

Confession is for everyone, every day.

We all need to confess, and we need to do it every day (Matt. 6:12). No one is so bad that he or she is beyond forgiveness. Scripture includes murderers (Moses) and schemers (Jacob) and adulterers (David) among God's people so that no one can say that they are beyond the reach of God's mercy.

On the other hand, no one is so good that only one or two confessions a year will do. There are things we could confess from any moment in our day, because no one is perfect this side of heaven.

So even though sin weighs a lot, we aim to see it and enjoy the benefits of confession. When we lay it down, we are thankful and find joy in confession, knowing we are already forgiven because Jesus has become our sacrifice, once and for all (Heb. 10:11–14). Our greatest need has been met.

Discussion and Response

1) Practice saying, "I am a sinner, saved by grace."
2) How do you hope to grow in confessing sin?

We Are Needy

Life Is Hard

Our Hearts Are Busy

Hard Circumstances Meet Busy Hearts

Sin Weighs a Lot

Say "Help" to the Lord

Say "Help" to Other People

5

Say "Help" to the Lord

In C. S. Lewis's book *The Horse and His Boy*, Shasta endured a long journey in which nothing seemed to go right. As all hope was fading he noticed a quiet presence, breathing "on a very large scale." The barely audible breathing was Aslan's, the God figure in the book, who had been accompanying the boy through many of his difficulties.

"Who are you?" asked the boy.

"One who has waited long for you to speak," responded Aslan.[5]

So far we have identified the two struggles of humanity: hard circumstances and hard hearts. And we have touched on how our response to both is to speak to the God-who-hears. Now we will settle into that response even more.

We Need to Pray (but We Resist It)

It is not always easy to talk openly to the Lord. We need help, but it is difficult to actually ask God for it. Why is it so difficult? Why do we sometimes resist speaking to him?

Take anxiety as an example. Anxious people know they are needy, but their instincts are to worry their way through doomsday scenarios so they can be prepared. Meanwhile Scripture urges us to pray rather than to feed anxiety (Phil. 4:6).

Our inclination is to live self-sufficient lives. When there is trouble, we first try to figure it out, then we worry, as if there is no one who cares or hears. Or maybe we give God the cold shoulder because he didn't give us what we had hoped for, or we hide from him because we cherish sins in our private world. There are probably dozens of reasons why we resist calling out to the Lord.

I know I resist asking for help. I prefer to give help and to keep my neediness to myself. This means that I am slow to ask both other people *and* God for help. That is deranged, indeed. But I am not alone.

God indicted all of Israel by saying, "They do not cry to me from the heart, but they wail upon their beds" (Hos. 7:14).

Wailing on our beds is easy and natural. But crying out to the Lord is spiritual—it is a gift from the Spirit—but it is also the most human thing we can do. Real life begins with, "Help, I need Jesus." Listen to how the psalms cry out to God:

> Incline your ear, O LORD, and answer me,
>> for I am poor and needy. (Ps. 86:1)

> O LORD, God of my salvation;
>> I cry out day and night before you.
> Let my prayer come before you;
>> incline your ear to my cry! (Ps. 88:1–2)[6]

We have no reason to resist. Humility before our Father, rescuer, and comforter; openness and freedom to speak what is on our hearts to Jesus, who calls us his friend—these are spiritual fundamentals.

Pray the Prayers of Scripture

From this starting point of humility, we can imitate the disciples and say, "Lord, teach us to pray, as John taught his disciples"

(Luke 11:1). Then we can be tutored by the two hundred or more recorded prayers of Scripture. Think of these prayers as open doors into our deepest needs. Here are some of the prayers we find:

Prayer for Help in Trouble

"Help" in times of trouble will be one of our favorite types of prayers. Psalm 130 begins with the direst of pleas:

> Out of the depths I cry to you, O LORD!
>> O Lord, hear my voice!
> Let your ears be attentive
>> to the voice of my pleas for mercy! (vv. 1–2)

Dire straits are best accompanied by "help." We have a basic *need* to cry out, "Help."

In the psalms, the request is often for deliverance from enemies who threaten to destroy the entire nation. In Psalm 130, the entreaty is more personal. The psalmist is teetering between life and death, and God invites us to speak the same words when we are in overwhelming and threatening situations. Either way—"help" for yourself or for your community—this is one of the ways that God teaches us to call out to him.

What form will this deliverance take? This is a question for which we, indeed, need help, because it doesn't always look the way we expect.

A child dies two days after birth. Her parents cried out for help, and hundreds of friends cried out too. Might there still have been deliverance? Consider that the parents had been delivered from death and the Evil One and that the child belonged to God and would be with him. Those deliverances might not lessen the parents' and friends' grief, but they do mean that the community can grieve with hope.

There are mysteries in deliverance, but since God has identified himself as our savior or rescuer, we are confident that we will see deliverance, even if it looks different from what we first expected.

Prayer of Confession

"Lord, forgive me" is certainly one of the important prayers of Scripture, and we aspire to make it one of our favorites.

Forgiveness of sins is essential to human satisfaction. The Hebrew word for that satisfaction is *shalom*, which means that all is right before God, and when all is right before God, we experience an abiding peace that is unruffled by the disappointments of life. Only confession and forgiveness bring *shalom*.

We have a *need* to confess sin. When we confess sin and couple our confession with an accurate knowledge of God's mercy, we can expect nothing short of a growing peace.

Psalm 130 begins with a plea for deliverance. The desperation is palpable. He needs help quickly. Yet notice where his mind goes:

If you, O LORD, should mark iniquities,
    O Lord, who could stand?
But with you there is forgiveness,
    that you may be feared. (vv. 3–4)

The psalmist knows that if there is no forgiveness of sins, there is no deliverance. Since there *is* forgiveness of sins, he is confident that nothing will separate him from the loving presence of his God, and if God is present, all is well.

His need for confession and forgiveness is his deepest need. Once that need is satisfied, the psalmist continues his prayer with a declaration of his patient endurance. After all, when we are assured of God's faithful love, we can be sure that we will see

God's goodness, so we can wait patiently. From that declaration he turns to his brothers and sisters and assures them of God's faithful love.

God's gracious forgiveness makes his name great. No one else, real or imagined, claims to forgive sins like he does, so we are pleased to say, "Forgive us our debts, as we also have forgiven our debtors" (Matt. 6:12).

When in doubt, confess something. Confess that you are struggling to pray, if needed. Confession is always a good place to start when we feel lost.

Prayer to Know the Lord Better

When God's forgiveness takes hold of us and begins to transform our experience of everyday life, the door opens to surprise us with even more of God's character. Who is this God who loves and forgives?

Notice the back and forth. The hardships of life provoke our prayer for help. Confession and forgiveness assure us that God will, indeed, help. Then our hearts are deflected from our circumstances and toward the Lord himself.

Psalm 46, for example, envisions the worst but doesn't even ask for help. Instead, the psalmist knows that his greatest comfort lies in remembering who God is:

God is our refuge and strength,
    a very present help in trouble. . . .
The Lord of hosts is with us;
    the God of Jacob is our fortress." (vv. 1, 7)

The psalmist's comfort is the knowledge of God.

For the psalmist, this knowledge was bound to God's promises and past faithfulness to Israel, especially in the nation's exodus from Egypt. For us, this knowledge is summarized in Jesus.

His death and resurrection assure us of his love, forgiveness, presence, and faithfulness. He is the deepest satisfaction to the real needs of life. On some level we have always known this. We have anticipated that our needs are ultimately resolved in a relationship. We have known that love has something to do with it. But we haven't always understood how Jesus is that relationship.

The apostle Paul certainly understood. He was rejected by people he loved, he lived with a chronic health problem, he had been shipwrecked more than once, and he was under house arrest. But he was at peace because his deepest need—to know God—had been met (e.g., Phil. 4:12).

Paul had Jesus, which meant that he had everything—life, love, fellowship with the Father and the Spirit, and all good things. With Jesus in view, his troubles, though extreme, felt transient and less burdensome (2 Cor. 4:17–18).

This knowledge of Jesus is especially important during suffering. At those times Satan raises questions about the character of God and suggests, at least, that God stands opposed to our best interests. If our knowledge of God is weak, we are left with a god who is a strange composite of truth, satanic lies, our projected desires and expectations, our experiences with our parents, and the accumulation of life's hurts. This is not the God of the cross who loved us while we were enemies, and this composite will not sustain us.

In other words, all suffering raises a relational question: Does God love me? So we pray to know him accurately and better (Eph. 1:17; 3:17–19). As we do, we aim for rest, because resting in him is a way to honor him.

> For God alone my soul waits in silence;
>> from him comes my salvation.
> He alone is my rock and my salvation,
>> my fortress; I shall not be greatly shaken. (Ps. 62:1–2)

Practice Praying

What we are trying to do is have Scripture shape the way we pray. To this end, we can highlight the prayers in Scripture and make them our own, but there is no reason to limit ourselves to the prayers of Scripture. Instead, we can make everything in Scripture a prayer. For example, every command in Scripture becomes an occasion for confession—"Lord, I fall far short, please forgive me"—and a request for power—"Lord, give me power to follow you fully." The phrase in Psalm 62 about finding rest in God can be prayed as our aspiration: "Father, this is what I want—to rest in you alone. Please teach me that you alone, not my ability to figure things out, are my rock and rescue."

Scripture takes us from circumstances to matters of the heart. Poor health, fears about those we love, financial stability in an unpredictable economy—Scripture takes these seriously and deepens them.

Prayer for our sick aunt will include her circumstances (physical health) *and* her soul. We will pray for healing, and we will pray that her inner person is renewed, especially through knowing God's presence, while her body will never be fully renewed in this life.

Prayer about our selfish boss will include petition that the boss will act justly *and* (1) that we will be able to work knowing that Jesus himself is our boss (Eph. 6:5–6), or (2) that we will find opportunities to trade kindness for the boss's selfishness (Eph. 4:32).

Prayer for an out-of-control schedule can include (1) confession of wanting to please people (people pleasers are always saying yes); (2) confession of an obsession with video games; (3) faith to take a weekly Sabbath; or (4) grace to focus on what is in front of us as we trust God for the things yet to do.

We move from things seen to things unseen, circumstances to spiritual realities.

So we start with a simple "help" to the Lord. That is the hardest step. It is impossible in ourselves, which means that when we say it, we can take pleasure in God's power at work within us.

And then a universe of communication possibilities opens up to us. Every cry of our hearts can be further shaped by Scripture. We cry out, God reveals more of his heart to us, we learn of him and speak more, he reveals himself more, we respond in thanks, and on and on. We need this communication, and we look forward to praying this way with others.

Discussion and Response

1) How are you like Shasta, not speaking to God?
2) That rhythm from seen (personal circumstances) to unseen (spiritual realities about God and what he is doing) is an important one. How will you practice this? Ask other people how they do it.

We Are Needy

6

Say "Help" to Other People

Keep in mind where we are going. We want to help each other well. Since needy, humble helpers are the best ones, and our own neediness actually serves other people, we are practicing the basics of being spiritually needy.

We are moving from feeling needy, to knowing our deeper needs, to asking the Lord for help, and now to asking others for help. Each step becomes more difficult.

Given the relentless difficulties of life, the competing voices ready to interpret those difficulties, and those sin weights that we might not even see, we pray, and then we ask others to pray too. We need to do this, because if we jump right in to helping others without revealing our own neediness, we put humility at risk. It only takes a few seconds to recognize a slick consultant who merely dispenses answers in contrast to one who is needy before God, has walked a similar path of transparency, and now sits humbly with us, side by side.

Ask for Help

Asking people for help makes calling out to the Lord seem easy by comparison. The Lord already knows we are weak and needy, but other people? That is a different story. They may not know, and we desperately want to appear competent before them. Even though spiritual neediness is one of the most attractive acts of a human being, we have our own views of strength, honor, and what is most becoming, and pleas for help are not on that list.

But it really should be simple.

The apostle Paul wrote, "Brothers, pray for us" (1 Thess. 5:25; also 1 Cor. 1:10–11; Eph. 6:19–20; Col. 4:3). Apparently, he was no longer embarrassed by his weakness and need. Paul was thoroughly schooled in rejection and humiliation. He was once a noted up-and-coming Pharisee, and then—he became nothing. He was nothing before his Hebrew kin, and he was of no reputation before many of the churches he founded. Having learned that Jesus made himself of no reputation before others, Paul was unconcerned about his own reputation. That is how he was able to ask for prayer.

If we desire to be perceived as competent and in control, we will not ask for prayer. If we know that humans, by nature, are spiritually needy, and God's plan is that we turn both to him and to other people for help, we will ask for prayer.

How to Ask

Whether we have never asked anyone to pray for us or we do it every day, the goal is to grow both in how often we ask for prayer and how we ask for it.

How often? We want to ask more than we do now.

How to ask? We want to ask for prayer about both circumstances and matters of the heart that sit below the surface, for things seen and things unseen. We take the skills we have learned in personal prayer and ask others to pray with us.

First, we put our burdens into words.

Second, we attach words of Scripture that capture both our real needs and God's purposes and promises. That is, we pray for what we know our Father wants to give us. Here are some examples:

- First, the burden: "I have been so tired. I feel like I am always a few steps behind on everything."
- Second, we attach Scripture: "Would you pray that I would rest in Jesus?" The Scripture that shapes this prayer is from Matthew 11:28–30: "Come to me, all who labor and are heavy laden, and I will give you rest. Take my yoke upon you, and learn from me, for I am gentle and lowly in heart, and you will find rest for your souls. For my yoke is easy, and my burden is light."

- First, the burden: "This is so hard. Would you pray for healing for my daughter?"
- Second, we attach Scripture: "Would you also pray for perseverance and that I would be able to fix my eyes on things that are not seen?" (Heb. 6:11 and 4:16–18).

- First, the burden: "I have been so impatient with my kids recently. I need help."
- Second, we attach Scripture: "Would you pray that I will know Jesus's unlimited patience toward me so that I will pass that on to my children?" (1 Tim. 1:16). Or, "Would you pray that I will see my anger as *my* problem and not theirs? I want to see that anger is murder and the problem is that I demand something and am not getting what I demand" (James 4:1–10).

- First, the burden: "Would you pray that I will find work?"
- Second, we attach Scripture: "And would you pray that I will trust the Lord for manna each day rather than get swamped by my anxieties?" (Matt. 6:28–34).

And sometimes our request for prayer can be very simple and desperate: "I feel undone. Would you pray for me? I don't feel that I can pray for myself, and I don't even know what to pray."

If you have prayed for someone, you know it is a privilege. Other people will feel the same way when you ask them to pray for you. Once we get the knack of asking, we can ask for help for some of our other burdens in life, such as looking for a job or cleaning up an apartment. We can even let people know our financial needs.

Recognize Help When It Comes

Once we've prayed and asked others to pray for us, all that's left is to keep watch. We assume that if we pray according to God's promises, we will see him on the move. So we wait expectantly, and then we acknowledge his work when it comes. Here are some ways to do that.

Build Monuments

Knowing the human tendency to forget the mighty acts of God, the Israelites built monuments (Josh. 4:1–7). After the Lord stopped the waters of the Jordan so the people could cross into the Promised Land, the Lord told Joshua to gather stones from the center of the Jordan and establish an enduring reminder of what he had done.

When we recount with our community God's answers to our prayers, we are laying spiritual monuments that we hope will have more endurance than mere stones. We hope they build up the body of Christ on earth.

Say "Thank You"

One New Testament version of a monument is "thank you." When Jesus healed ten lepers, only one returned and thanked him (Luke 17:11–19). That one was also the only one assured of the more complete healing that comes when we turn to Jesus as our rescuer instead of merely our physician-consultant: "Then Jesus answered, . . . 'Rise and go your way; your faith has made you well'" (vv. 17–18).

Say "thank you"—to God and to other people. The independent and self-sufficient never say this. The arrogant think they deserve whatever good things they receive, so they never say this. But the spiritually needy who know that the Lord has lavished his love on them (Eph. 1:8; 1 John 3:1) are quick to say "thank you."

And we aim our thankfulness at spiritual matters—what is permanent and certain, from the Spirit, rather than temporary. *Spiritual* means that we peer through the things seen so we can see the things unseen. It includes forgiveness of sins along with all the other benefits and fulfilled promises we have in Jesus and through his death and resurrection.

Notice why spiritual matters deserve priority in our thanks. We should be thankful for physical health or for a job following a season of unemployment, but if our thankfulness is grounded on only those things we can see with our eyes, which do not have longevity, we will, someday, have *no* reason to be thankful, because someday we will be unhealthy, and suddenly we can turn from thanks to bitterness.

Proclaim His Faithfulness

Whatever our monument might be, we want it to be public, even if the *public* is one friend. The psalmists were experts at these things. They would cry out to the Lord in the midst of their miseries and recount his faithfulness, and if they could not notice God's faithfulness from the day's events, they would review Israel's past, stake their confidence on how he had forgiven sins, and then speak publicly about his faithfulness (Ps. 130:7–8).

The Psalms highly value words that are spoken. We can know good things about the Lord, but the psalmists challenge us to turn knowledge into speech, both to the Lord and to others. The kingdom of heaven is by no means quiet. When we have good news, it should be announced.

Our task is simple: ask for prayer and then let those who have prayed for us know what God has done. It is simple, but it is also a powerful intrusion of the Spirit in the everyday life of the church.

Discussion and Response

1) How have you said "help" to others?
2) How will you say "help" to others?

Part 2

We Are Needed

Looking back. We are needy. The goal is to become transparent and humble friends who are at ease with our neediness. We see our hardships and sin, speak openly about them to the Lord, and are willing to ask others to pray for us.

Looking ahead. We are needed. This is the way the church moves forward—through mutual love and care. Such expression of love was less obvious in the Old Testament, when people relied on kings, leaders, and prophets, but when the Spirit was given at Pentecost—everything changed. Suddenly, ordinary people had extraordinary impact.

The goal is to grow in a long list of skills. These skills, however, will enhance the basic things we already know and do every day: we move toward others when they are in need, we get to know them, and we pray.

We Are Needed

Remember: We Have the Spirit

Move toward and Greet One Another

Have Thoughtful Conversations

See the Good, Enjoy One Another

Walk Together, Tell Stories

Have Compassion during Trouble

Pray during Trouble

Be Alert to Satan's Devices

Prepare to Talk about Sin

Help Fellow Sinners

Keep *the* Story in View

7

Remember:
We Have the Spirit

I had been keeping my recent fears to myself. My wife knew, and she was helpful, but a good rule of thumb is that when you are stuck in hardships or sins, you keep enlarging the circle of those who know until you are no longer stuck. I think this is a good rule, but I had decided I could get through it on my own.

My wife and I were out for a meal with some friends when they asked, "How are *you*?"

In the most casual way possible, I said, "Oh, I've been experiencing some odd fears lately."

Our friends stopped, as if to put all other conversations aside, and considered my fears with me for the next half hour. Then they prayed for me.

Why was that so helpful? Good helpers, such as these friends:

- are present, which is a good thing when fears arise;
- listen, really listen;
- draw you out;
- avoid being impersonal teachers;
- never minimize, are never trite;
- remember.

Those are qualities of Jesus himself, and they are some of the skills we will consider up ahead.

And, on that particular evening, I don't know exactly what these ordinary people did that was most helpful, but they did have impact. My fears lessened from that meal on. One thing I do know is that my helpers were qualified by the wisdom of the Holy Spirit.

You Have the Spirit

Everything changed when Jesus came. He died for sins, rose from the grave, and then, at Pentecost, sent the Spirit. The professional religious caste was no longer the titled few. Now followers of Jesus have all the competencies needed to encourage and instruct each other (Jer. 31:33–34).

That is the reason we even consider helping others. We live in the age of the Spirit. Apart from Pentecost, we would be referral agents who simply introduce needy people to the real experts. We would hold our tongue for fear that we would just make matters worse. With the Spirit, we move toward other people and are amazed that God uses ordinary people to do his kingdom work.

Having the Spirit does not mean that otherwise blank minds suddenly become streams of profound insight and comfort to those in need. We remain fully capable of saying stupid and hurtful things. But it does mean that our ability to help will bear the marks of the Spirit, such as patience and kindness (Gal. 5:22).

The Spirit Gives Wisdom

The Spirit gives us the wisdom of God. This wisdom overlaps with wisdom that we can gather from books and careful observations, but it goes deeper. It is wisdom rooted in the cross and the resurrection of Jesus. It is crammed with guidance from the Father through Christ—wisdom that we could never discover on our own (1 Cor. 1:20–25).

When we are feeling utterly worthless, for example, we can ignore it, debate it, or succumb to it. The best wisdom of the world can't get us much further. In contrast, the wisdom of God reveals that worthlessness is about our connections. We are connected to things that have been forced on us, such as the sins of others, or we are connected to things we love, such as work, hobbies, or even the people who love us. It turns out that none of these things are sufficient in themselves to make us whole. The deeper wisdom of God reveals that, by faith, we are connected to Jesus, and then we investigate that wisdom for the rest of our lives in order to understand Jesus more fully.

As Jesus is with us through the Spirit, his wisdom becomes a part of us. This wisdom brings the truths of the cross into the details of daily life.

- God's wisdom leads us to serve others.
- God's wisdom shows us how to forgive those who sin against us.
- God's wisdom makes unity with God and others possible.
- God's wisdom inspires us to take action when there is injustice.
- God's wisdom helps us understand suffering. As the King goes, so we go. Since he was not spared the cruelties of the world, we should not expect to be spared.
- God's wisdom assures us of God's love. While we were enemies, he loved us. This is the only evidence strong enough to comfort and assuage the inevitable doubts about God's goodness. We trust in the one who loved us and express that faith in love toward others (Gal. 5:6).

The wisdom of God is condensed in Christ and him crucified. If you know that wisdom, you are eminently qualified to help others.

The Spirit Works in Ordinary People

And there is just one other qualification. It is this: you are an ordinary person. God has determined that run-of-the-mill people do most of his work—not professionals, not experts.

But habits die hard. A woman was having problems with her children, and she needed help. She was in a small group—she could talk to an (ordinary) person there. Her church had a pastoral staff—she could ask one of the pastors. She also knew a very smart Bible scholar—she could ask him. As a good American, she chose the scholar. Within a minute or two, and bored out of her mind, she began to realize that the kingdom of heaven doesn't move forward by mere knowledge.

We have no complaints about knowledge, and there certainly is a place for expertise, but we aren't necessarily going to want help from the person who has access to the most information. We want help from someone with godly wisdom, and that wisdom, which resides fully in Jesus, is in the public domain. A child can understand it, while a scholar might be sitting in the dark. It seems to be a questionable way to change the world, but it's God's way.

> For consider your calling, brothers: not many of you were wise according to worldly standards, not many were powerful, not many were of noble birth. But God chose what is foolish in the world to shame the wise; God chose what is weak in the world to shame the strong . . . so that no human being might boast in the presence of God. (1 Cor. 1:26–29)

What a fine strategy. If the beautiful, rich, and talented were the ones who had spiritual power, we would revert to the class structures that have cursed humanity from the beginning. The *haves* would lord it over the *have-nots* and take pride in themselves, as if they were fully responsible for their power and blessings. But when ordinary people are used in ways they did not even know, then God is honored. The woman having problems with her children would probably have done better to talk to a wise mom in her small group.

Are you feeling ordinary or a little less so? Do you have the Spirit? If so, you are just the person God has been looking for. When you, in your weakness, move toward others, you honor God and are more powerful than you know. You are qualified by the Spirit.

Discussion and Response

1) What are the qualifications of those who have helped you in your times of trouble?
2) What did your helpers do that was most helpful?

We Are Needed

Remember: We Have the Spirit

Move toward and Greet One Another

Have Thoughtful Conversations

See the Good, Enjoy One Another

Walk Together, Tell Stories

Have Compassion during Trouble

Pray during Trouble

Be Alert to Satan's Devices

Prepare to Talk about Sin

Help Fellow Sinners

Keep *the* Story in View

8

Move toward and Greet One Another

With the basic qualifications fully met, off we go.

We could start by erecting a small booth in the church narthex, like the one Lucy staffed in the *Peanuts* cartoon, and put out a sign saying, "Psychiatric Help 5 Cents." That way, we could help our friends and even make new ones.

Yet there are a few problems with this. One is that no one would come for help, even if we lowered the price, because most people do not ask for help. Even desperate people are slow to ask for help.

So we take the initiative and move toward each other. God has moved toward us; we move toward others in his name.

God Moves toward Us

God always takes the initiative. Even when Adam and Eve were exiled from the garden, he followed them into their exile. Watch him pursue his people, as symbolized in the relationship between Hosea and Gomer—a marriage between a prophet and an adulteress wife (Hos. 1:2). When God's people run from him as Gomer did from Hosea, God moves toward them and cares for them as Hosea did for Gomer.

Better yet, watch Jesus. He relentlessly pursued and invited the marginalized and outcasts to be with him.

Our picture of kings is that they are cordoned off from the public, like the Ming Dynasty emperors of China living in their Forbidden City. In contrast, our King does not simply leave the castle door ajar, so a brave subject can enter unannounced. He goes out to the people in everyday garb and personally invites them to stay with him. Jesus is God in the flesh, who stepped down from his throne and entered into the affairs of daily life. In doing this, he removed all boundaries and barriers between him and us.

God comes to us—that is grace, and it starts cycles of grace through the body of Christ.

We Move toward Others

As the King goes, so go his people. He moves toward people; we move toward people. He moves toward people who seek him and people who do not; we move toward those who want help and those who seem distant and marginalized. He moves toward friends and even enemies; we move out beyond our circle of friends to those far beyond that circle.

Imagine how this can transform our churches. Instead of talking to the same people—those with whom we are comfortable and who are similar to us—we treat others as God has treated us. Imagine how aloneness could gradually be banished.

It sounds great, and it is fun to imagine, but it is so difficult to practice, which is as it should be. If it were easy, we could simply do it. But since it's hard, unnatural, and, at times, impossible, we are driven back to, "Jesus, help."

Make no mistake: to move toward others is hard. There are some people we don't click with, some we don't like, and some who have wronged us. It is good to move toward others, but it is not easy.

We Greet One Another

Let's say we actually made it and are face-to-face with a real person. Then what happens? The thought of awkward silences and feeling a little stupid puts this entire plan in jeopardy. What do we say?

We start small. We greet the person.

Greetings are not a form of politeness from a bygone era. They are skills that imitate the Lord, they show respect and kindness to others, and we are meant to grow in them. Listen to one of Paul's greetings:

> All the brothers send you greetings. Greet one another with
> a holy kiss. (1 Cor. 16:20)

We don't have to kiss someone when we greet them, but when we move toward others, we are to greet them with familial warmth. Since we have been invited, welcomed, and greeted by the Lord,[7] we have the opportunity to reciprocate. By welcoming the least, we welcome Jesus (Mark 9:37).

There are, however, so many people we could greet. Even in a small church, there are too many people to greet personally. We don't aim to become serial greeters who offer a brief and boisterous "Good morning," then move to the next person and offer the same greeting.

Consider whom you are greeting. They are children of the King, your brothers and sisters. Some might feel lost, which is all the more reason to greet them. Others might be seeking something but are unsure *what* that is, and we have the privilege to invite them to a place that could be home. Others we have seen before, but we don't yet know their names.

Greetings, of course, take time. This means our greeting list might be short, because we have a finite amount of time when the church is gathered—or when a friend is walking by on the street. We cannot greet everyone. So here is how we prioritize:

- The visitor (what Scripture calls the "foreigner" or "alien") comes first.

- The visitor who returns comes next.

- The less popular, the introverts, the marginalized, or those sitting alone come next.

- Then come the children. Jesus singles them out as examples of the marginalized.

- "Hi, _____" is offered to as many people as possible, which doesn't have to be accompanied by a hug or a handshake.

Good friends are interspersed through these greetings, but they are left for later if time is short.

A reasonable application of Scripture is to greet one person we don't know or don't know well every time we gather with others in the body of Christ.

And if we feel a little awkward? All the better. Some people are naturals at moving toward others, greeting them and striking up a conversation. Most of us are not. So we pray that we will share in this feature of God's character. We move toward others, not because we can do these things with ease but because of Jesus.

Discussion and Response

1) Sheer willpower might not get us very far, even in something as simple as moving toward others and greeting them. A better way is to consider how God does this with you. How *does* God move toward you?

2) How do you plan to act on the call to move toward others?

We Are Needed

9

Have Thoughtful Conversations

Once the greetings are over, the pleasure of knowing someone begins. This means having thoughtful conversations—ones that go below the surface niceties. We don't aim to draw out problems so that we can be helpers. We are simply interested in knowing another person, which is a basic feature of everyday love.

It doesn't always start well though. There you are, in front of someone you don't know.

"Good morning. My name is Susan."
"Hi. I'm Naomi."

And then . . . nothing.

This seems to happen more often with men than women, but the thought of it is enough to keep you among safer relationships.

Or maybe you notice a person who seems to keep a distance, so you go over and introduce yourself.

"Good morning. My name is Bill. I don't think we've met."
"No."
"Welcome to our church. Have you been here before?"

"No."

Hmm, he seems perturbed, but you decide to keep trying, and you search for a question that could elicit more than a yes or no.

"Are you from around here?"
"Yes."

So much for a better question.

"Okay . . . I just . . . wanted to say hello."

Very awkward, but don't let it discourage you from moving toward him and those like him. As you do this in the name of Jesus, you are doing a fine thing. Success is measured differently in God's kingdom. And who knows? Maybe he'll keep coming to church, and after another dozen greetings, he might begin to trust you with a few more details.

Knowing and being known—by design we enjoy human connections, and those connections are forged over time through normal interactions and questions that gradually ask for more. Such connections are the foundations for mutual help, and they are helpful in themselves since they are expressions of love.

Think of the best conversations you have had. They probably included give and take, keen interest from both parties, talking about things that are important. Our aim is to learn from those conversations and duplicate them whenever possible.

Following are some ideas about how to have these thoughtful conversations.

An Initial Script

During a first greeting, we usually have a few prepared remarks and stock questions:

"I don't think we have met. I'm Joe."

"Have you been here before?"

"Have you lived here for a while?"

Subsequent conversations have their standard lines too:

"Nice to see you again. How have you been?"

"How 'bout those Phils?"

"Beautiful weather, isn't it?"

We can locate those questions in the X-ray from chapter 1 among the various rings or concentric circles. Those rings identify the events, circumstances, and influences in our lives.

There are many other questions:

"Married?"

"Any kids?"

"What kind of work do you do?"

"Are you going away this summer?"

"What are you doing for the holidays?"

"Where do you live?"

"Where did you grow up?"

"What's happening in your life?"

"Everyone in your family healthy?"

These are fine questions, but, like appetizers before a good meal, we don't want to get filled up on them, because they ask for nothing personal. Good conversations go a little farther.

Follow the Affections

We hope to learn what is important to the person we're talking to, which is another way of saying that we hope to hear what is on his or her heart. The way in is to listen for what is dear, what is loved, what is feared, what is hard—we listen for how someone feels. For example, we certainly want to know the age and names of someone's children, but we also want to hear stories about the children that reveal parental affection, hopes, or griefs.

Have you ever had an initial conversation or one early on in the relationship in which the one with whom you were conversing was emotionally flat throughout?

"Are you going anywhere this summer?"
"Yes, we usually spend time with my husband's family."
"Do you enjoy your time with them?"
"It's okay. That's what we always do."

Now what? A bland response gives you very little direction. It leaves no room for follow-up. So you are left looking at each other, or you change the subject.

We listen for signs of life. A question about the holidays might reveal the pleasure or pain of gathering with extended family. A question about health can reveal thankfulness or fear. So we keep our ears open for details that are important to someone. This may sound clinical, but it's not. It's what you do naturally when you are interested in someone. You follow the affections. You follow what excites, what is prized, and what is hard.

We want to know others, but we can't know them by simply amassing the events of their lives. Personal knowledge is what we go after. When we hear Scripture say that God knows us (e.g., Ps. 139:1), it means that he knows our pleasures and griefs, loves and loathings, and he has us in his heart. How do we do this for someone we are trying to move toward? We do it by asking questions that get at what matters.

"What did you do this week?" That question gets information.

"How are you?" This question gets closer to the heart.

There are two versions of the *how* question. The first is a mere greeting that does not anticipate an answer other than a reflexive, "Fine. How are you?" The second version is revolutionary, and some people have never been asked it. When someone responds with a perfunctory "Good," or "How are *you*?" you can respond with, "How are you, *really*? How has your week been?" Now we are getting personal. We can even dust off those other questions that sought only surface information and aim for deeper knowledge that way.

"How is work [really] going for you?" A superficial response, such as "Good," now becomes, "I am concerned about budget cuts and the future of my position."

"How is school?" A response such as "Almost over" can be followed up with, "Has there been anything you have especially enjoyed?" or "Any plans for next year?"

"How are your children?" Children are always important to parents, so you'll be sure to hear something about a person's heart with this question. And a parent will love you for asking.

We listen for likes and dislikes. We listen for feelings and emotions because they reveal hopes and fears. And we listen for God's place in it all.

Mere information can be boring. "I woke up, had a bagel for breakfast, took a shower, drove to work . . ." Blah, blah, blah. If the conversation threatens to stay in information purgatory, just bust in when there is a pause.

"And how are *you*?"

We move into another person's world, walking side by side. We want to be moved by the things that move her. Then, having her on our heart, we pray for her or ask how we can pray for her.

Prayer

Once we pray with or for someone, we are in the ongoing story of his life, and it is an honor to be there.

We hear information.

We hear what is important to him and let that settle into our own heart.

We pray for him.

Then we follow up the next time we see him:

> "I've been thinking about your son. I am praying he would not be defeated by the failure he feels in school and would keep talking about it with you."

> "I have been praying for your relationship with your boss and that you'll have patience, wisdom, and confidence that God is with you. How is it going?"

All this might seem to be help at its most minimal, and, in one sense, it is. Up to this point, we have not given hours of time. We greet one week, ask a few follow-up questions the next. It doesn't seem like much. But those who receive even this minimal care from someone are blessed.

Knowing others well enough to pray for them—that's help at its most basic and at its best.

Discussion and Response

1) We can all grow in conducting these daily and more intentional conversations. How do you hope to grow? What will you do in order to grow? Who comes to mind? Who will you get to know better this week? How will you do it?

2) Who in your life is one step ahead of you in knowing people? What does that person do?

We Are Needed

Remember: We Have the Spirit

Move toward and Greet One Another

Have Thoughtful Conversations

See the Good, Enjoy One Another

Walk Together, Tell Stories

Have Compassion during Trouble

Pray during Trouble

Be Alert to Satan's Devices

Prepare to Talk about Sin

Help Fellow Sinners

Keep *the* Story in View

10

See the Good,
Enjoy One Another

As a general rule, we will not be able to have growing relationships in which we help other people unless we see the good in them, and they know we see good in them. Would you listen to someone who helps you merely out of duty rather than love? Would you listen to someone who doesn't really like you? God has determined that help takes place in the context of love and respect. Enjoyment can sum it up—do you enjoy the other person?

The apostle Paul did this well: "I give thanks to my God always for you because of the grace of God that was given you in Christ Jesus" (1 Cor. 1:4). That is how he begins his first letter to the Corinthians. It is the way he starts *every* letter. What makes this letter unique is that the recipients were bad. They boasted in their reputation and associations, ignored the poor among them, and were known for being divisive. Yet even in all their badness and their disrespect for Paul, he could see the Spirit working in them. He could see the good in them, and he enjoyed it.

Such an attitude can lead to deeper conversations:

"Let me tell you more about the grace I have seen in you."

"Somehow you remain hopeful in hard things. How do you do it?"

"You have been given amazing gifts, and I have been praying that God would protect you so you can continue to use them well."

"I have been thinking about you recently."

If we were to receive such thoughtful comments, we'd be willing to open up to the one who spoke them, numbering him or her among those we call first in times of struggle. Paul teaches us something very important in this regard—he didn't let the bad overshadow the good. He was able to affirm the good and encourage his readers in the faith. We want to do the same.

The goal here is to keep our eyes open for good things in others. When we see good things, we savor them and point them out. As you get to know people, you will encounter many hard things, some unattractive things, but if you also see good, you will see people more as God does, and that is a blessing.

Look for the Good

All humanity has been created in God's image (Gen. 1:27). Though sin has distorted and sullied that image, the image persists and is the reason we can enjoy each other (James 3:9). Everything good is a reflection of the God who is good. The following story is an example of what can happen when you look for the good.

A wife had had enough of her husband's lies, lewd comments about other women, drunkenness, and self-admitted narcissism. She asked to see the pastor of the church she attended; and her husband, who mocked her profession of faith, was willing to go with her.

Why did he see the pastor? He said that he was certainly not going to change, but he wanted to "help her be happier. I love her."

The pastor saw the bad. The husband's sin was flamboyant. And most people would quickly forgive the pastor if he had jumped up and strangled him. However, the pastor entered a different way. He saw the humanness—something of God's reflection in him. He saw how the man was affected by his wife in his simple willingness to come and seek help with her, and that is good.

"You are a hybrid if I ever saw one. You are hard as can be on the outside but softer on the inside than you let on. Thank you for coming."

The pastor was soon brought into some of the difficult and painful things in this man's life.

Just keep heading toward the heart. It is the repository for our emotional life, and good comes from its springs. Keep looking until you see the good, and you will see it.

Notice Character Qualities

Be eager to discover patience, self-control, humility, kindness, selfless acts, encouraging words, attentiveness, courtesy (which is a form of respect), interest in justice and the marginalized, hard work, and love. These refractions of divine goodness are best identified, praised, and enjoyed. If their appearance is episodic and brief, and even if they are contaminated with selfishness or pride, don't let the unattractive features of someone's life blind you to the good.

Her house is a mess, and her friends assume she will be late. Many find her frustrating and unreliable. But those who know her see more. When help is needed, she is there and usually on time. When you speak with her, she is all there.

She hears you, anticipates where you are going, is moved by what you say, and will pray for you more than will five other friends.

Love is able to see past the clutter of a disorganized life.

Other evidence of the good in people is easy to see but only if you have access to some behind-the-scenes details.

He is never too busy to help. A two-hour drive to pick up a stranded member from his church was the most recent interruption to his very full days. As he recounted the trip to a friend, it was clear that he'd enjoyed every moment of it, even though he'd been out quite late the night before. This good was recognized because the friend with whom he shared the story took the time to ask for a few more details.

Notice Gifts and Talents

Everyone has strengths, and these strengths are good. They can be used selfishly, but they are also gifts from God that are expressed in the way we serve one another.

You can probably identify your friends' gifts rather quickly, including strengths in organization, administration, music, teaching, parenting, math, reading, mechanics, aesthetics and decorating; planning; computer technology; electronics; construction; empathy; and athletics. Here's one:

She was a teen stereotype—piercings, tattoos, a low-grade sneer, and a commitment to seem uninterested in church. No adult had any point of contact with her.

The children in the church like to run among the pews after the service. One Sunday a two-year-old, who tends to be part of this pack, strayed and went for the steps. The toddler could navigate the steps, but the tattooed teen was unsure about that, so she quickly followed to make sure the little girl was okay, trailed her in her wanderings, and then escorted her back to the main room.

A parent noticed this and went over to the teen, saying, "Thank you so much for how you cared for that little one. You are very kind. But you'd better be careful. Soon all the kids will want you as their big sister."

From that moment on, you could watch the teen brighten and relax whenever that parent stopped to say hi.

Just keep looking. You will see something good.

A high-functioning autistic young man can remember many people's names and birthdays and past conversations. If you were to meet him, you would think he hadn't noticed you, because he always looks away. Little would you know that you had found a place in his heart and that he will remember the details of your conversation the next time he sees you.

The church is an ideal venue to see the talents and gifts of others, because most gifts emerge in the context of serving people.

Notice Pleasures and Preferences—Even Hobbies

Whereas character qualities and even innate gifts can go unnoticed by those who possess them, pleasures and preferences are what others consciously enjoy.

Listen for what excites them. When we hear people talk enthusiastically about almost anything remotely good, we are brought into their pleasures and can find ourselves enjoying them too.

And if they enjoy something we find uninteresting? Out of respect, we believe they enjoy that something for a good reason, so we will ask a few more questions.

"Why do you like watching baseball so much?"

Yes, we like something just because we like it, and sometimes people can't give reasons for their preferences. But if we ask, we might get something more.

I knew someone who had a preference for Diet Pepsi that bordered on obsessive, and he always seemed a little cranky if I drank something else when Diet Pepsi was available. For years I attributed it to an eccentricity, until I asked why Diet Pepsi seemed so important to him.

"My older brother, who died when I was eight, drank Diet Pepsi."

That is an admirable preference.

With baseball, you might hear something similar:

"I enjoy watching it with friends."
"I enjoy the statistics and the camaraderie of being in a virtual league."
"When I was a boy I would watch it with my father, and it makes me feel like I still have a connection to him."

Now we are getting somewhere. Sports can be about relationships, or it can be about admiring physical skills or appreciating strategy. When you follow others' interests and pleasures, you might begin to enjoy what they enjoy or at least the reasons why they enjoy it.

Notice Spiritual Vitality

As enjoyable as all those are, more direct expressions of faith in Jesus Christ are even more so.

A friend asks you to pray for her.

A person tells a story about turning to Jesus in the midst of great weakness.

Someone confides in you about a struggle with anger and asks for help.

A spouse says, "I was so encouraged by Scripture this morning. Could I tell you about what I read?"

Immediately after a church service, a friend greets you and mentions specific ways that she was challenged and encouraged by the morning's sermon, and she asks for your thoughts as a way she can learn even more.

A friend told me about his favorite sermon. It was ten minutes long, and he recounted it word for word. The result was a double gift. He enjoyed remembering it, and I was spellbound. The next day I sent him this note: "Thanks so much for the sermon. Now it is among my favorites, and I will quote you when I pass it on to someone else."

All of us can see the good in our friends. Scripture, however, authorizes us to see the good and enjoy it in all people, even when most of us are not always so good. This will encourage others, increase our affection for them, and make it much easier to talk about things that are hard.

Discussion and Response

1) Whom do you enjoy? Have you told those people why you enjoy them?
2) Have you recognized the good qualities of someone in your life but not told them what you see? What might you say?

We Are Needed

11

Walk Together,
Tell Stories

Once you have seen good things in someone, you will want to
walk with that person side by side. The greetings and conversations we've considered so far could be done in five minutes or less,
after a church service, at a child's baseball game, or while bump-
ing into someone at a store. The privilege of going further into
each other's lives will take a little more time. That time could come
from accumulating minutes before and after church services in
which you gradually move a conversation to even deeper matters,
or it could come by extended times over coffee or in a small group.

Short conversations become longer ones and longer ones require new skills, and if we are to help others we need to grow
in these skills. The Christian life is about growth. Everything is
in motion, drawn along by our knowledge of Jesus Christ and
the Spirit's power. Conversations and relationships move forward too. They grow, they deepen, they become more loving,
encouraging, and helpful.

Ask for Stories

One privilege of a growing friendship is to hear our friend's
story. Scripture itself is the story of God, and we know him

through that story. So it is no surprise that we learn about others through their stories.

We like to tell our story, and we like to hear other people's stories.

Short Stories

We have already been hearing short stories:

"What did the doctor say?"
"Tell me about what happened at work."
"How was your vacation?"
"How was your time with your sister?"
"How did you end up in this area?"

The more important the short story is to the person telling it, the more details you want to listen for.

Long Stories

Listening to the long stories might require a shared meal.

"How did you become a follower of Jesus? The longer version, please."

A woman once came to our house for dinner. She had been coming to the church we attended but had remained on the periphery. She was quiet, almost shy, but could become testy in a moment.

We asked if she would tell her story. Specifically, we wanted to know how she came to know and follow Jesus.

The story began innocently enough. She had traveled in her mid-twenties, as if searching for something. Eventually the words of a street preacher rang true, and she came to Jesus with her burdens and followed him. She knew her life had changed. The preacher then urged her to move in with him in order to be properly "discipled." The mentoring, however, meant that she was enslaved by him for the next eight months, only to escape to a different part of the country when he started getting clumsy in his control. She had been hiding the story for the last ten years, and telling it to us was her coming out.

We were blessed that she would entrust us with such a story. The reason for her distance from others was suddenly clear, and we immediately made the connection that her anger came out only when spiritual leaders from our church, though well intended, reminded her of an earlier time. As a result of her opening up, both my family and the church were able to include her with more wisdom, patience, and love.

She was blessed as she became known and was brought into the community; we were blessed to know her and be brought into her life.

Stories about how someone came to know Jesus are the best, yet there are other, longer stories that are also important:

"How did you get into this kind of work?"
"Tell me about the family you were raised in."
"How did you meet your spouse?"
"What have you learned in marriage?"

It doesn't get much better than hearing someone's story. Knowing and being known. Openness. A growing friendship. And as we grow in these things, we should expect this general rule: the better you know other people, the more you enjoy and appreciate them—that is, the more you love them. And the more you love them, the more you will be invited into their lives during hardships.

Caution: Avoid Matching Stories

As we walk with each other, we gradually accumulate a list of do's and don'ts. The following is one of the don'ts.

Your friend: "You won't believe what happened to me the other day. I was cleaning out a gutter and put my hand right into a bee's nest. I was stung five times on one hand and once in the face. The neighbors thought I was going crazy when they heard me."

You: "That's amazing. I hate bee stings. I get stung every spring and fall, no matter what. Last fall we had these really small bees in our grass that stung me every time I went by. I must have been stung ten times. I thought I would end up at the hospital."

Many conversations consist of one telling a personal story and the other matching that story. This isn't wrong. We want to know and be known, and swapping shared experiences is one way to do it. But we don't want to communicate, "Okay, enough about you, let's talk about me." Instead, we want to draw out another: "What happened next?" Otherwise, your friend will feel that you really didn't hear her story and may be reluctant to share other, harder stories with you.

Follow and Draw Out What Is Most Important

Love naturally moves to what is important in someone's story and follows up. With the bee story we could ask, "And how are you doing now? The stings still bothering you?"

When we care about someone, we are alerted by what is most troubling, most exciting, most anticipated, and most desired. We listen even more carefully when strong emotions such as anger, fear, shame, sadness, and grief are evident. We might notice word pictures. Terms such as *weighed down*, *drowning*, *darkness*, *alone*, and *walking on air* will tell you a lot.

If you are listening to a longer story and want to be sure you understand key features, try to identify an event from the story that, in one episode, summarizes the significant things in your friend's life.

Can you identify turning points? The most influential characters? Where the past has left its imprint?

Follow up when you notice such things. It could be a short comment: "You really love your dad." It could probe: "That move in seventh grade seemed to be a huge change for you," or, "Could you say more about your grandmother? She seemed really important to your story."

Do you notice any regrets? Anything your friend would want to do over? Scripture is certainly concerned about guilt, both its causes and cure. And guilt, for whatever reason, tends to strangle spiritual growth. So we follow up on that when we get the slightest whiff of it.

When you don't know what is important in someone's story, just ask: "What is most meaningful to you about this? What is the hardest part of this problem for you?"

All such questions serve as a reminder that the stories of those you love are interesting and important. So we listen carefully for clues, draw people out, and partner in both joys and burdens.

Discussion and Response

1) What have you appreciated when you have heard other people's stories?
2) What would you like people to know about your own story?

We Are Needed

12

Have Compassion during Trouble

We move toward others.

- We greet them.
- We have short but meaningful conversations.
- We gradually discover what is important to them.
- We begin to pray for them.
- We see the good. We like them. We enjoy them.
- We have longer conversations.
- We continue to pray for them.

Those ordinary steps are reminders of how to be a friend rather than profound insights about helping. We all can do them. They are easy and ordinary.

The risk is that their very ordinariness might cause us to judge them as second-rate ways to care for one another. But the truth is that following these steps is powerful enough to reach into our souls. When people have practiced just one or two of these steps on us, they have left their mark. That's because every step has the imprint of Jesus, so you can be sure that each one will be fruitful.

Now notice how relationships naturally progress from there.

When you follow what is important to someone, that path will take you to the primary struggles of life: suffering and sin. Suffering is the trouble that comes *at* us. Sin is the trouble that comes *out of* us. In the next few chapters the goal is to draw from Scripture some ways that God speaks to both of these daily troubles so that we can speak to them too.

A person's struggle with sin might take precedent and become the focus of our conversation. If someone confides in you about an indulgence in porn or cruel anger, it will grab your attention. But even there, we might talk about the hard things that preceded the specific sin before we focus on the sin itself. We typically talk about our hardships with each other before we talk about our sin.

Compassion

> "We will never be the same. We always knew that losing a child was one of the most severe blows, and it has been worse than we could have imagined, but God has given us enough grace to get through each day."

Their thirty-year-old son had died in a motorcycle accident only two months earlier. It was nothing reckless, no drugs or alcohol. A lone deer had wandered into the road.

In the face of such news we must do something. The pain we hear is rightly answered with a compassionate response. That means we love those who suffer to the point that we are affected by their hardships. In a sense, compassion is enjoyment's companion. We enjoy the good things in someone and have compassion during the hard things.

Compassion Grieves with Those Who Grieve

No blank looks, no change of topic. When we hear the hardships of those we love, we find them a place in our heart such that we too are not quite the same. "Oh, I am so sorry. This is so hard and painful. It tears away at me to hear about this"—those words might seem dramatic or extreme, but they are apt words of compassion from a loving friend.

We search for words to express compassion. Compassion can be expressed in deeds, but the overall culture of God's family is expressive. We speak to God and to each other, and we do it often. The wisdom in this is obvious to those who are troubled, because silence is usually interpreted as indifference.

"I am so sorry," "I am with you in this"—that's what we want to communicate.

Compassion Remembers

If we are affected by someone's suffering, we will remember it, which is one of the great gifts that we give to each other.

A young man's father died, and his local church, as we would expect, loved him well—invitations to dinner, a high priority on everyone's prayer list, and warm e-mails, texts, and cards. After a week or two, the generous care began to taper off, also as we would expect. The few people who still asked the young man how he was doing stood out to him as unusually caring.

A year later, on the anniversary of the father's death, a friend from the church called and left a message: "I remember that your father died on this day last year. I just wanted you to know that I was thinking about you and prayed for you. I prayed that there will be times today when the memories you have of him bless you."

The young man was stunned. He was changed. He was comforted and encouraged, and he committed to keep others on his heart long term.

God's premiere self-description is "the compassionate and gracious God" (Ex. 34:6 NIV). This means that both our pain and our prayers affect him, and he has us on his heart. He takes our burden on himself and remembers us. As we imitate our Father, we want to feel the burdens of others too.

> Bear one another's burdens, and so fulfill the law of Christ. (Gal. 6:2)

So we call, e-mail, track down the suffering at church. We have them on our heart, and we want them to know it.

Say something. Do something. Remember. That is the basic idea.

What Not to Say

Yet the call to say something does not mean that everything we say is good and helpful. It's important to know what *not* to say. Sometimes we may be tempted to respond to someone's suffering with thoughtless platitudes. Here are three offenders.

1) Do not say: "It could be worse."

Believe it or not, that is only the first half of a hideous comment, for example: "It could be worse—imagine if you broke *both* legs."

We have some odd ways of cheering each other up.

The comment is accurate—everything *could* be worse. We suffer and then, along with the suffering, have a comforter who says it could be worse.

Such a comment is utterly thoughtless. God himself would never say or sanction it. God does not compare our present suffering to anyone else's or to worst-case scenarios. Ever. If we hear friends do this in their own suffering, it does not give us the right to chime in. Instead, it might be a time to warn them.

> "Yes, your suffering might not seem as severe as _____, but God doesn't compare your sufferings to others."

If we make such comparisons, we might be tempted not to speak of the suffering from our hearts to the Lord because we would consider it whining, which it certainly is not.

So even though things could be worse, that is never an appropriate thing to say to others or to let others say about their situation. God is not dismissive of our hardships, and neither should we be.

2) Do not say: "What is God teaching you through this?" Or, "God will work this together for good."

Those platitudes are biblical in that God does teach us in our suffering, and he is working all things together for good (Rom. 8:28). We agree with C. S. Lewis when he writes that pain is God's megaphone to arouse a deaf world. But these kinds of comments have hurt so many people; let's agree that we will never say them.

Consider a few of the possible problems with this and other poorly timed misuses of biblical passages:

- Such responses circumvent compassion. Will you have compassion if someone is being "taught a lesson"? Not likely.

- Such responses tend to be condescending, as in, "I wonder when you will finally get it."

- Such responses suggest that suffering is a solvable riddle. God has something specific in mind, and we have to guess what it is. Welcome to a cosmic game of Twenty Questions, and we'd better get the right answer soon; otherwise, the suffering will continue.

- Such responses suggest that we have done something to unleash the suffering.

- Such responses undercut God's call to all suffering people: "Trust me."

In our attempts to help, we can overinterpret suffering. We search for clues to God's ways, as if suffering were a scavenger hunt. Get to the end, with the right answers, and God will take away the pain. Meanwhile, the quest for answers is misguided from the start and will end badly. Suffering is not an intellectual matter that needs answers; it is highly personal: Can I trust him? Does he hear? Suffering is a relational matter, and it is a time to speak honestly to the Lord and remember that the fullest revelation he gives of himself is through Jesus Christ, the suffering servant. Only when we look to Jesus can we know that God's love and our suffering can coexist.

3) Do not say: "If you need anything, please call me, anytime."

This heads in a better direction; it is not quite a platitude. However, this common and kind comment reveals that we do not really know the person. Sufferers usually don't know what they want or need, and they won't call you. The comment is the equivalent of, "I've said something nice, now see ya later." It gives no real thought to the sufferer's needs and circumstances, and the suffering person knows it.

Instead we could ask, "What can I do to help?"

Or (better) we could consider what needs to be done and do it.

Wise friends buy more dog food, do the dishes, drop off a meal, cut the grass, babysit the kids, clean the house, give a ride to small group, drop off a note of encouragement and then another and another, help sort out medical bills, and so on.

Any such acts of love and service make life easier for the suffering person. And a meal is never just a meal; maid service is never merely a timesaver for those served. These acts say to the sufferer, "I remember you"; "I think about you often"; "You are not forgotten"; "You are on my heart"; "I love you." The time we give to creative strategizing is the power behind such acts. It is unmistakable love that mimics the strategic planning of the triune God's rescue mission. He planned and acted even before we knew our real needs.

The oddity of our clumsy and sometimes hurtful attempts to help is this: we have clear ideas from what has helped us in our suffering, but we do not adopt it when seeking to love others. We do not always speak to others in the way we would like to be spoken to.

Proceed Humbly and Carefully

Compassion offers some protection from foolish words. When we love others, have entered into their lives, and have been moved and grieved, we stand a good chance of offering words or deeds that encourage. But proceed with care. Job's comforters took their time and seemed to care for him. They were moved by his troubles, but they still said things that were wrong and unhelpful, and even right and unhelpful.

With this in mind, when we are in the presence of those who are suffering, we walk humbly with them before God. Scripture gives us a number of insights into human suffering, but no insight is exhaustive. The mystery in suffering reminds us that we are still like children who don't fully understand the ways of the Father.

Humility asks, "What can I do today that would help you?" Then it might make a few suggestions so the person doesn't flounder or wonder if you mean it. (Can I watch the kids today? Do you need a ride to your treatment? Do you have plans for dinner?) If the person declines, accept it, but do not end the conversation without an offer to pray. Ask what he needs prayer for and either pray right then or pray later and then follow up the next time you see him. That is compassion.

Our Theology Shapes Our Compassion

We speak foolish or unhelpful comments because we do not always love well, but also we speak them because we misunderstand biblical teaching about suffering. Our beliefs can facilitate compassion or be impediments to it. Here are some common but wrong beliefs:

- Low-grade suffering is common; you just deal with it. Really bad suffering means you have done something really wrong, and God is displeased.

- We all have hardships, but our good Father will give us the ability to bear it, which means that it won't feel that bad.

- We all have hardships. Christians have them a little less than their pagan neighbors.

- We can praise our way through it.

- Think of those worse off than you and be thankful.

Each one of those beliefs yields well-intended but hurtful words because we have the story wrong. It is so important that we get the story of suffering right.

Here is one way of telling the story. Suffering reminds us that the world and everything in it, including us, are not quite right. Everything will not be right until Jesus returns and his will is done on earth as it is presently done in heaven. So we are people of hope. We look ahead, yet we also know that Jesus's incarnation changed everything, even now.

In the Old Testament, suffering and trouble were usually a result of the people's disregard for the Lord. There were exceptions such as Job, who went through the worst of sufferings yet was the best of men, and in that, he pointed to Jesus. But, overall, trouble was the result of people's sin, so we can understand why we might think that good people are trouble-free and bad people are not.

Then the perfect Son of God suffered with us and for us, and, with his resurrection, which was the Father's approval of the Son's life and death, our understanding of suffering was forever revised. Suffering is part of the Father's plan. For those who follow Jesus, we expect to experience the sufferings that are common to all humanity—accidents, health crises, pain from broken relationships—and we expect even a little more because we follow the suffering servant. All our hardships are now ways that we participate in the sufferings of Christ. He suffered with the world; we suffer with it. Our endurance in hardships shows our solidarity with him.

The Father does indeed mature us through hardships. We notice the wisdom of those who have endured through trials, and we are struck by the immaturity of those who try to keep suffering at bay through drugs, alcohol, porn, or some other self-soothing tactic. But we don't make a one-to-one connection between a particular sin and a particular hardship. Jesus himself matured under hardship; we will too.

As we suffer, our hearts are exposed. We can see where we put our trust: in people, money, pleasure, and power—or in God. But that is a benefit of suffering, *not* necessarily the cause. We are tested daily by trouble and hardship, as royal children always are, and we expect these trials to grow faith rather than kill it.

The belief that is hard to shake is that the Father wants to make our life easier and that he is eager to shield us from the hard things of life. This, of course, is *not* the case. When we get God's story right, our suffering confirms that we belong to him; it does not mean that he is distant and unresponsive. Suffering is a time when he is most obviously at work, and our spiritual task is to turn to him rather than try to manage our world our own way. Endurance in suffering doesn't grab our attention, but it is a response so important that it will have value that lasts beyond death.

Meanwhile, we look ahead to the time when everything will be made right. Christ will return, sin will be vanquished, death and everything connected to it will be dismissed. We will experience bodily resurrection and will live in peace with the triune God and with his people.

Since there are so many other ways to tell the story of suffering, we practice the correct one, read Scripture's various retellings, and read the accounts of wise people. As we grow in compassion, we need this story so that it can be translated into words. The better we understand it, the better our help will be and the deeper our compassion for those with hardships.

Discussion and Response

1) When have you witnessed compassion?
2) What is your growing list of do's and don'ts with those who are suffering?
3) How do you tell Scripture's story of suffering?

We Are Needed

13

Pray during Trouble

We move toward those who are hurting and put compassion into words:

> "I want you to know that you've been on my heart."
> "I've been so saddened by what's happened."
> "I think about you often. How are you? This has been a heavy, heavy burden."
> "It might not seem like much, but I am with you in this. I feel the burden and have been praying for your comfort."

Time to Pray

Then we return to that familiar ground: God is at the center of all our swirling emotions, and the most human thing we can do is speak to him. Now we bring that practice into the troubled life of a friend. Our best question will be this: "How can I pray for you?" Or simply, "Let's pray *now*."

With this simple suggestion, it is as if the universe opens before us. A two-dimensional conversation—between you and another person—goes three-dimensional. We come alongside the sufferer and bring God and the suffering together. We bring light into claustrophobic darkness, where our friend might be alone and without hope. We remind her that God hears. We revisit the promises of God. And we do all this in a way that leads with compassion. That simple call to prayer is crammed with spiritual realities.

Since it is so crammed, expect this request to be awkward at times, or hard, or impossible. Spiritual battles, previously in the background, now show themselves, which means we might find ourselves praying that we could say, "Let's pray now." But if we have practiced asking for prayer, we have already known spiritual power.

How to Pray

Once we are willing to pray with someone, *how* we pray is easy. We pray for what is on our friend's heart—we pray for what is especially important to him or her. We know how to pray, and we also expect to grow in how to pray.

One way we will grow is in how we connect with what is on a friend's heart with apt themes and passages in Scripture (see chapter 5). Whenever we ask for prayer, and whenever we pray, we work to match what is on our hearts with what is on God's heart. Here are more ways to do that as we consider prayer for healing, comfort, and faith.

Prayer for Healing

Prayer for healing is the most frequent request. We ask for prayer when we are sick or when someone we love is sick:

"How are you?"
"My aunt is sick."
"Oh, what's wrong?"
"Her arthritis is giving her a lot of pain."
"Let's pray for her now."

"Okay."

"How should we pray for her?"

"We could pray that her arthritis will be healed."

So you pray for healing, which is consistent with how God teaches us to pray (James 5:14).

But even this simple prayer request has much more to it. You see something good. This niece clearly loves her aunt, so you ask more about that relationship, because good things always invite more attention.

"Tell me more about her. You must really care about her."

Then you can ask if your friend sees or talks with her aunt. If so, you can go deeper. What does your friend say to her aunt? Is her aunt a Christian? What Scripture has your friend shared? What Scripture might be encouraging?

And you always have that most powerful form of help—persevering in prayer and following up with your friend.

"How's your aunt been? I have been praying for her. Has her pain subsided?"

Do that once or twice, and your friend will be blessed and will take notice of your love and will soon be asking you to pray for things that might be more difficult to share. And all you have done is pray for her aunt. God uses ordinary means to do his extraordinary work.

If prayer for an aunt is as personal as your friend gets, you move to, "And how are *you*?"

People also want to pray for healing for themselves. Here again we typically move from circumstances (the actual sickness) to things that are deeper or spiritual ("Who is Jesus?" and "How do we turn to him?"). Sickness is always a spiritual matter in that it raises questions about God's care and goodness, and it is an opportunity to grow in trust and obedience. Notice how the apostle Paul writes about physical suffering:

> Though our outer self is wasting away, our inner self is being renewed day by day. For this light momentary affliction is preparing for us an eternal weight of glory beyond all comparison, as we look not to the things that are seen but to the things that are unseen. For the things that are seen are transient, but the things that are unseen are eternal. (2 Cor. 4:16–18)

Paul moves from his physical difficulties—outwardly wasting away—to deeper spiritual realities.

So, as we ask someone how to focus our prayer, we can also ask questions such as these:

> "How is your faith in the midst of this? I know that sickness always reveals faith struggles for me. It shows me that my faith in Jesus is more wobbly than I thought."

> "The apostle Paul says that our troubles are outweighed by the glory that is just up ahead. That's what I will pray—that future glory will outweigh the pain you feel right now."

We are eager to pray for what we are asked to pray for, but we also expect that Scripture will take those requests and further shape them.

Prayer for Comfort

Along with healing, prayer for comfort is common. Prayer for God's comfort extends to all kinds of suffering. We honor God when we know his comfort. It shows that he is great, so we are pleased to pray for it.

> Blessed be the God and Father of our Lord Jesus Christ, the Father of mercies and God of all comfort, who comforts us in all our affliction, so that we may be able to comfort those who are in any affliction, with the comfort with which we ourselves are comforted by God. (2 Cor. 1:3–4)

We pray for comfort, and after we know that comfort, we can pass it on to someone else in times of trouble.

When we pray for comfort for someone, we pray specific prayers whenever possible. "Please, Lord, comfort Mary" is okay, but what kind of comfort is Mary asking for? When possible, we ask her what comfort she hopes to receive from the Lord.

Comfort might mean simply that the storm of suffering would lessen, or it might mean that the suffering would be increasingly outweighed by the knowledge of Christ and what we have in him (2 Cor. 4:16)—or both.

We pray, and then we follow up and ask if our friend has received comfort. If comfort is slow in coming, we pray especially that spiritual benefits would outweigh the hardships. The greatest of these comforts, of course, is that because of Jesus's death and resurrection, our God will never leave us or forsake us. Only our sins could separate us from God, and those sins have been paid for once and for all in Jesus. This is the best comfort.

As comfort comes, the Lord has blessed two people—both the one who prayed and the one who received comfort. Together they have witnessed the love of God and the Spirit's power. That is how God builds his church.

Prayer for Faith

Prayer for comfort eventually merges with prayer for faith. That is, comfort leads us back to the promises and presence of God, which we know by faith. Our friend might not ask us to pray for this, but Scripture keeps leading us to the best things.

When we pray for faith, we pray to be able to see clearly and trust more fully. Without such vision, perseverance is impossible.

> "Lord, please give my friend eyes to see spiritual realities in her suffering."

That is one loaded prayer for faith. In it we are assuming that there are two ways of seeing. One way is with the naked eye. We open our eyes in the morning and see chaos, mounting storms, loved ones in trouble, and sins galore in a world that seems to be getting worse. The other way to see is with our eyes of faith. We open them and see *past* what our senses detect to the love of God—because why else would Jesus die for us when we were acting as his enemies (Rom. 5:10)? We see that suffering is not the last word, but hope is. We see that God has purposes in hardships, and the grandest purpose is that we would trust him rather than be fair-weather friends who trust only when we have what we want.

When we pray for faith, our hope is that someone will see through the immediate circumstances and into spiritual realities: God has rescued us, incorporated us into the line of the suffering servant, has forgiven our sins, is so near that he dwells within us, and will give us power to believe, hope, and even love in the midst of the trouble.

Faith sees beyond the morass of our present sufferings. It sees that suffering has a purpose.

> We rejoice in our sufferings, knowing that suffering produces endurance, and endurance produces character, and character produces hope. (Rom. 5:3–4)

Faith sees that we are people in motion, on a journey, led by the Spirit.

> Let us . . . lay aside every weight, and sin which clings so closely, and let us run with endurance the race that is set before us. (Heb. 12:1)

People facing trouble do not always ask for prayers to strengthen their faith, but a helper knows that this prayer will bless them.

> "I know that hard things can sometimes put our confidence in Jesus at a low ebb. How are you?"

> "How have you been doing spiritually during this?"

> "I will pray for your comfort and also for the Spirit to give you eyes to see Jesus and what Jesus gives you. Do you have any ideas of what specifically I could pray that the Spirit would give you?"

Though these are ordinary things to ask for, such prayers will push you toward matters we talk about too rarely. Many of us have never gone beyond the casual "How's school?" "How's work?" The movement toward things that are explicitly spiritual can seem like quite a jolt. It might feel risky or even impolite. But we need this in our own hardship, and others need it in theirs. We know our deepest needs, and to reach for anything short of these is unloving. When we pray for faith, we are praying for what is most important.

Pray for Everything

We pray for whatever is on someone's heart: a job, a debt, a child's school performance, a dating relationship, and so on. We pray for everything. And if we cannot immediately see how

Scripture extends and reshapes the request, we simply pray for what the person asked.

But we remember, too, that we are children who do not always know what we need. When we talk to our Father, we know that he hears, and we anticipate that he will do more than we imagine. He is not limited by our specific request but answers in a way that's even better. In a similar way, we look to Scripture for ways to deepen and embellish our everyday prayers.

When we keep track of Scripture's prayers and the ways we can pray for each other, the list includes prayer for wisdom (James 1:5), unity (John 17:29–31), fellowship and encouragement (1 Thess. 3:10), love and discernment (Phil. 1:9–10), knowledge of God's will (Col. 1:9), perseverance (Col. 1:11), faith that lasts (Luke 22:32), fruitfulness (Col. 1:10), the fruits of the Spirit (Gal. 5:22–23), and the armor of God (Eph. 6:10). Any of these can be appropriate extensions to our daily petitions.

And Follow Up

Whatever we pray, we are zealous to know how God is working, so we follow up.

A married couple asked for prayer during a meeting with their small group. They were going to see their adult son in a few days. They hadn't seen him in over a year. Though he had rejected Jesus, which he knew was a burden for his parents, phone conversations had gone well, and he seemed to look forward to the visit. The parents asked the group to pray for conversations that would encourage their son and build their relationship.

That was a skillful request. As a result, the group was both taught about how to pray and honored to be brought into the parents' deepest concerns. It was their privilege to pray.

No one, however, followed up and asked about the visit.

The parents *did* follow up. At the next small-group meeting, they gave specifics about the day, which inspired the group to continue praying for the son and also demonstrated to the group that praying for someone includes identifying what the Spirit did with those prayers. You can be sure that over the next few months there will be a flurry of pastoral follow-ups in this group. "We prayed together for _____. How did it go?"

How many times do we pray for someone and then just check it off our to-do list? As a result, we miss what the Spirit has been doing. We miss the opportunity to either persist in prayer or give thanks.

In an age of social media and twenty-four-hour news cycles, we are constantly confronted with massive human needs, and we can be overwhelmed with the number of people to pray for. To follow up with them all would be impossible. As a way to prioritize the needs, it is best for us to focus on people we actually see, those we can pray *with*. Identify one person, then two, perhaps three. Growth proceeds in small steps.

Pray and follow up.

Pray and follow up.

Pray and follow up.

Discussion and Response

1) Have you prayed *with* anyone in need yet?
2) How could you follow up with someone today?

We Are Needed

14

Be Alert to Satan's Devices

When suffering knocks on someone's door, Satan too comes knocking. Life is a war zone, and Satan is the enemy strategist. He waits for those times when people are in the wilderness— vulnerable, desperate, and God seemingly far away or absent altogether. That's when Satan's questions about God's character, which might seem silly during the good times, suddenly make sense. Why would anyone entertain Satan's questions about God's goodness when everything is good? But a few bumps in the road, and our knowledge of God seems fragile, and that's what Satan is counting on.

We must therefore consider how Satan's devices affect how we help one another. Though Satan's power to enslave us was broken by the resurrection of Christ, he still has the power to tempt and accuse and confuse us. We need to be able to recognize it and know what to do.

Four Gardens

We can become alert to Satan's influence (and how to respond to it) by walking through four gardens depicted in Scripture:

Eden, the destitute garden of the wilderness, Gethsemane, and the resurrection garden. These four places were venues for battle, and they alert us to Satan's tactics.

Eden

Eden was a kind of proving ground for humanity. God tests his people, which is what kings do with their children. Otherwise, they never mature into their royal responsibilities. God essentially said, "You can eat here, but not there." Man's job was to listen to his words, believe him, and be faithful. Yet where God tests his children, Satan tempts (Gen. 3:1–5).

> "God isn't so good. How could a good father forbid you to eat from such a lovely tree?"

> "You and your desires are good. Follow your feelings. What you want is good. Why would God make you with those desires and then keep you from satisfying them?"

> "Life apart from God will bless you. Freedom means fewer restraints."

There is one more feature of Satan's strategies that comes after these initial temptations. Once we follow his lead, he condemns us: "You are so bad; God will never love and forgive you."

There he is in all his anti-glory, Satan, the accuser. He gets us coming and going. He promises freedom; he delivers slavery.

The man and woman were walking along, minding their own business. They heard a few comments and questions from the Interloper, and suddenly the tree looked good. Their logic was turned completely upside down, but it seemed to make perfect sense—they even thought they had seen the light. And this took place before the hardships of life could make them (and us) even more vulnerable.

Since these satanic strategies remain effective today, we engage against variations on these old tactics. Remembering what happened in Eden will help us be alert to how a sufferer is being tempted or accused by Satan, which leads us to the next garden.

Jesus in the Wilderness

By the time we get to the New Testament, Satan's temptations have faded from view. Why bother tempting when everyone already knows the outcome? Satan wins, the people turn away from the Lord, and the Lord perseveres with obstinate children and reaffirms his promise that there will be a future and better deliverance.

But then Jesus, the second Adam, walked out into a deadly wilderness, which is a garden cursed. He was showing us how to combat Satan's schemes. Where everyone else had failed, a new champion had accepted the challenge and was committed to changing the master story.

> The Spirit immediately drove him out into the wilderness. And he was in the wilderness forty days, being tempted by Satan. And he was with the wild animals, and the angels were ministering to him. (Mark 1:12–13; also Matt. 4:1–11; Luke 4:1–13)

Jesus then did what no one else had done: he trusted in the words of God and dismissed the lies of Satan, even when it meant more suffering and even death. Satan's strategies were variations on his old ways. He appealed to Jesus's senses—his desires—and he suggested that God the Father was the one who needed to be tested.

Although forty days without food, Jesus never wavered. He knew exactly how suffering works. Suffering has the old scent of rebellion in it. Whenever Satan smells it, he comes to stir up trouble and hover until the body is dead so he can claim it as his own.

Jesus was prepared and armed. He knew Scripture.

Now, since we have the Spirit, the Word, and prayer, we can be hopeful and stand firm against Satan as we go through our daily wildernesses.

Gethsemane

The next garden is a grove of olive trees where Jesus went with three of his disciples on the night he was arrested.

> They went to a place called Gethsemane. And [Jesus] said to his disciples, "Sit here while I pray." And he took with him Peter and James and John, and began to be greatly distressed and troubled. And he said to them, "My soul is very sorrowful, even to death. Remain here and watch." And going a little farther, he fell on the ground and prayed that, if it were possible, the hour might pass from him. And he said, "Abba, Father, all things are possible for you. Remove this cup from me. Yet not what I will, but what you will." And he came and found them sleeping, and he said to Peter, "Simon, are you asleep? Could you not watch one hour? Watch and pray that you may not enter into temptation. The spirit indeed is willing, but the flesh is weak." (Mark 14:32–38)

Spiritual battle reached its zenith in this garden. The Son of God was seemingly vulnerable. Whereas we are left to surmise Jesus's physical pain in the wilderness, in Gethsemane there is no guessing. This is the most intense suffering recorded in Scripture.

Suffering, we now know, is enough to summon Satan. Jesus certainly knew that, which is why he warned his disciples, "Watch and pray that you may not enter into temptation."

Jesus's counterattack? He prayed. Scripture and prayer are our primary means of doing battle.

He also tried to lead the disciples into battle. He had told them that Peter would disown Jesus and the other disciples would fall away. Prayer, in such circumstances, is more important than sleep.

A man neck-deep in suffering said, "I know that God says he won't give us more than we can handle, but I think he has given me more than I can handle." With Gethsemane in mind, we should hear, "Warning, warning." We are immediately compelled to rally around him and pray. Pray for power to know that his Father is with him, as he was with Jesus. Pray for power that he would be able to stand against Satan and his devices. Pray for more of the Spirit (Luke 11:13).

Gethsemane helps us know what to do when we see a spiritual battle raging in someone's heart.

The Resurrection Garden

The Gospel of John identifies one more garden, and the episode is heavy with allusions to Eden and its true gardener. It depicts a conversation between Mary and the resurrected Jesus.

> "Woman, why are you weeping? Whom are you seeking?" Supposing him to be the gardener, she said to him, "Sir, if you have carried him away, tell me where you have laid him, and I will take him away." Jesus said to her, "Mary." (John 20:15–16)

The true man—*the* image of God—stood firm in temptations, worked in this garden, and invited others to witness the final weapon against Satan's devices. The centerpiece of the garden is a tomb that is empty.

The resurrection is the evidence that Jesus truly was the

Son of God, and all the promises of God are now assured in him. His appearance in this garden shows that Satan has been defeated. Yes, we follow Jesus in suffering, but suffering does not have the final word. Jesus's resurrection leads the way to our own resurrection, and there is nothing Satan can do to stop it.

All is not well, however. We are given power and protection, but Satan is angrier than ever (Revelation 12). As a result, our vigilance, especially in suffering, is even more necessary than was the disciples'. Suffering is no time to sleep. It is a time to identify Satan's strategies and pray.

Our Strategies against Satan's Strategies

Satan still lies in wait, watching for hardships in our lives that just might leave us vulnerable to his lies. Scripture, prayer, and the assurance that we too will know resurrection with Jesus are our primary protection, so that's what we bring. Following are some examples of what you might say.

"How can I pray for you?" The question reminds us of spiritual realities, and prayer will always be an essential way to stand firm.

"Any questions *about* God or for him?"

"Satan waits for desperate times. Are there ways he's sneaking up on you? Any lies that he's tossing around?"

"'Be sober-minded; be watchful. Your adversary the devil prowls around like a roaring lion, seeking someone to devour. Resist him, firm in your faith, knowing that the same kinds of suffering are being experienced by your brotherhood throughout the world' (1 Pet. 5:8–9). Have you noticed the enemy?"

"As I was praying for you, I realized that Satan is such a fierce enemy. I am going to pray for comfort and healing for you, and I am going to pray that we are alert to his lies about God and lies about you."

"Satan will try to make your pain worse by suggesting that God does not love you. Let me pray that the Spirit would bless you with power to know God's love (Eph. 3:16–19). And we need ten other people who will pray the same thing."

"Despair usually has Satan's fingerprints all over it. We could do battle with a passage such as this one: 'So we do not lose heart. Though our outer self is wasting away, our inner self is being renewed day by day. For this light momentary affliction is preparing for us an eternal weight of glory beyond all comparison, as we look not to the things that are seen but to the things that are unseen. For the things that are seen are transient, but the things that are unseen are eternal' (2 Cor. 4:16–18)."

"Does this pain make you think that you must be guilty of something, and you have to figure it out? That's the kind of thing Satan does."

"Do you ever get angry with God? Satan is going to try to accuse you, but he's also going to use this as an occasion to accuse God."

"This is so hard, and Satan is such a persistent adversary. How can we pray?"

"Are you sure that you have forgiveness of sins in Jesus? Satan is going to suggest all this is your fault."

The apostle Paul kept this battle focused especially on forgiveness of sins. Notice from those comments above that Satan progresses from temptations to accusations. Armed with that strategy, he scans the church for times when the saints feel as though God is far away. At those times, he can work his ruse about us not being forgiven, but "we would not be outwitted by Satan; for we are not ignorant of his designs" (2 Cor. 2:11). And we need help in this battle.

Discussion and Response

1) Do you know people who are in this spiritual battle right now? How might you move toward them?
2) Read Ephesians 6:10–18. It is the best-known summary of our spiritual battle. As you read it, keep in mind that the apostle Paul is not introducing anything new. Instead, he is using spiritual warfare as a summary for everything he wrote in the letter. How might you pray, given this passage?

We Are Needed

15

Prepare to Talk about Sin

Next, prepare to talk together about sin. This tends to be the last thing we want to do. Who wants to talk about sin among friends? Suffering, yes. We can even see ourselves highlighting Satan's pernicious ways when someone is suffering. But to talk about sin? That seems so risky, so judgmental. When sin surfaces in another, we would much rather be silent and secretly judgmental than talk about it. We adopt a don't-ask-don't-tell policy, which avoids conflict and also protects us from being accused of sin ourselves.

Addressing sin is a tough one. How can we talk about sin with one another? Our church culture inadvertently communicates that preachers can talk publicly about sin, and a men's group convened to deal with pornography can talk about it, but as a general rule, it is impolite to talk about sin one to one.

We have already considered how the writer of Hebrews gives us a natural segue from suffering to sin (Heb. 12:1–2). He just assumes that normal human beings have sin that clings, and hardships are a time when that clinging is even more apparent. He doesn't wag a finger. He just makes a basic observation.

But it is still hard.

This chapter will consider *why* we talk about sin and how to approach those conversations. In the next chapter, we'll get more specific about what we say.

Why Bother?

Suffering and sin are the sum of human struggles. This means that we need one another in our struggle with suffering and in our struggle with sin and temptation. James wrote his final words on these very matters:

> My brothers, if anyone among you wanders from the truth and someone brings him back, let him know that whoever brings back a sinner from his wandering will save his soul from death and will cover a multitude of sins. (James 5:19–20)

"Save his soul from death" and potentially head off a future avalanche of sin—no one uses that kind of language with suffering. Suffering hurts more, but sin is more serious. Suffering will not last, but sin has consequences that reach into eternity.

In other words, when we put sin off-limits, we cannot defend ourselves as being polite people who merely avoid meddling. Rather, we are Pharisees who, during a leisurely walk, avoid eye contact with the dying person we almost trip over. We are neglecting matters of life and death.

But it is still hard. Dietrich Bonhoeffer said it well:

> The pious fellowship permits no one to be a sinner. So everybody must conceal his sin from himself and from the fellowship. We dare not be sinners. . . . The fact is that we are all sinners![8]

If we ignore our brothers' and sisters' sins, we have sinned against them, and we should ask their forgiveness. We need to move toward fellow sinners. We are family, after all, and we know the perilous nature of a life apart from God.

Examine Yourself First

To prepare ourselves to talk to people about sin, we look to grow in humility and patience. We'll start with humility.

Humility

Humility means that we already see our sins as worse than others' sins, so we have no reason to defend ourselves when someone points out our sin (Matt. 7:2–5). This does not mean that we must publicly identify our own sins before we talk about sins in others. It means that we live as redeemed tax collectors (Luke 18:9–14) who have no confidence in our own righteousness but live because of God's lavish forgiveness and grace.

Humility might be tested when you talk about someone's sin. The confronted person might say:

"Aren't you holier-than-thou!"

"Oh, and you have never done that?"

"Who are you to talk to me about such things?"

We can never predict someone's responses. Anger and defensiveness can come when we least expect it. In response, humility has nothing to defend:

"It's funny you should say that I should look at myself first. I have actually spent time doing that, and I saw that my own heart is a good bit uglier than I thought. And I really am open to you talking about my sins. We can do that now.

Then we can talk about what I was talking about earlier. I am trying to care for you in a way that I would want to be cared for."

"Am I saying things that are wrong or offensive?"

Humility is surprisingly sturdy in the face of anger. It includes a willingness to look at our own sins yet isn't diverted from our concern for another.

Patience

Patience is humility's partner. It is one of the identified fruits of the Spirit (Gal. 5:22), and it is a central feature of love (1 Cor. 13:4), so it is essential to our ability to be helpful. It means that the one we are speaking with is like us—he does not respond perfectly, he changes slowly, and he needs a patient helper.

There are times when patience is not the best course. Sometimes we act immediately because someone is in physical danger. If we hear of a child abused or a wife threatened, we have to do something, and the first step is to get help from the larger community. More often, however, sin is a danger to the sinner more than it is to other people, and patience is the order of the day.

"I was thinking about our conversation last week. I know I brought up something that was hard and isn't easy to face. Could we talk about that?"

Patience does not think, "If I were she, I would be working harder on this." Patience is interested in what direction people face. Do they face toward Jesus? Patience is more interested in direction and less interested in how fast people are changing.

A simple way to keep track of your humility and patience is to check for your own anger and its many variations, such as low-level frustration. When anger is present, humility and patience are absent.

See the Good and the Hard—First

When we talk to someone about his or her sins, it is, indeed, risky. What we hope to do is minimize the relational risks through love and wisdom.

As a general rule, we want to see the good in others and their hard circumstances before we see the bad. That seems wise, and it fits the style of the apostle Paul's letters.

See the Good

We already talked about seeing the good (chapter 10, "See the Good, Enjoy One Another"). Have you ever pointed out the facets of the character of God you see in someone? We tend to be slow to do that, and if we are considering how to talk to someone about sin, those good words are even less likely to come up.

You might be wise to postpone any talk about sin until you have spoken words that build up (though talking about sin, done well, should certainly build up). This is a good policy with family and others we live with.

Be careful though. Most of us don't need justification for postponing a conversation about sinful actions. Sometimes we should speak sooner about sin rather than later. When uncertain, keep in mind that our aim is to speak respectfully, in love, and to build up—whenever we speak.

Acknowledge the Hard Circumstances

If we see a friend lash out at her children, we have certainly witnessed her sin, but we might lead our approach with what is hard in her life.

"It seems like you are really stressed this morning. How are you doing?"

Parents do this often with their children. After a child throws a brief tantrum, you might hear a wise parent say, "Honey, I am going to get you a snack now. Sometimes you get hungry after playing all afternoon."

The parent is not ignoring the tantrum—she can raise the matter during the snack. Instead, she is identifying the hard circumstances of life and knows that these are times when the child is vulnerable.

This is also a way to approach an angry adult:

"Everything okay? You were really angry the other day. I don't think I've ever seen you like that."

"Everything okay?" and "How are you doing?" open the conversation to circumstances of life that might be especially difficult. I can remember seeing sinful actions coincide with the anniversary of a loved one's death, a stroke, a shocking medical diagnosis, and suspicions of a spouse's infidelity.

We believe that our sins can have mitigating circumstances. For example, killing in self-defense is not the same as murder for revenge. A tired child might be better served by a nap rather than a rebuke. Sin can be provoked by the hard things of life, and, as a general rule, we acknowledge those circumstances before we move on to the sin itself.

One at a Time

Here is one more principle: we don't have to talk about every sin we witness or suspect. Just deal with one.

Hatred stirs up strife,
> but love covers all offenses. (Prov. 10:12)

Above all, keep loving one another earnestly, since love covers a multitude of sins. (1 Pet. 4:8)

Those passages talk about covering sin and are tricky to interpret. They at least tell us that we do not have to confront every sin. Tensions appear throughout the body of Christ every day. If we raise every slight against us, we will only increase those tensions.

The Lord does not wave all our sins in front of us, and they will not be waved in front of us for eternity. When we cover a sin, we participate in this unique feature of the gospel. Rather than speak to the sinner, sometimes wisdom means resting in the Spirit to do his work. At such times, we can learn more of the good in someone's story and witness how love is more powerful than sin.

"Be patient with them all" (1 Thess. 5:14). That is the nonnegotiable. Humility and patience are essential for speaking about sin or covering sin.

Discussion and Response

This is a challenging task and worth a few extra questions.

1) Have you ever been confronted about your sin in a way that was edifying and fruitful? What made it helpful?
2) Have you ever been confronted about your sin in a way that was unedifying and hurtful? What made it so?
3) When might you cover rather than confront a sin?
4) Are you willing to talk to someone about sin?

We Are Needed

Remember: We Have the Spirit

Move toward and Greet One Another

Have Thoughtful Conversations

See the Good, Enjoy One Another

Walk Together, Tell Stories

Have Compassion during Trouble

Pray during Trouble

Be Alert to Satan's Devices

Prepare to Talk about Sin

Help Fellow Sinners

Keep *the* Story in View

16

Help Fellow Sinners

This much is clear.

Sin is our most dangerous problem.

The Spirit, the Word, and the community are God's primary means of doing battle with sin.

Though we prefer to live and let live when it comes to sin, we know that God has called us to help one another face our sins.

Human beings flourish when we do battle with sin rather than surrender to it. "He chose us in him before the foundation of the world, that we should be holy and blameless before him" (Eph. 1:4).

Sin is best raised in the context of faithful friendships where hardships have been shared and friends have prayed with each other. Now here are some occasions to speak up about sin:

- When someone faces temptations.
- When we have seen sin.
- When someone discloses and confesses sin.

When Someone Faces Temptations

To be human is to experience temptations. That is certain. We also know that we take only a short step from temptation to desire and then from desire to sin. Here are some friends who might be particularly vulnerable:

- Those who often travel overnight.
- Those who have lots of time alone or unaccounted for.
- Those who have a history of addictions or are taking an addictive substance such as narcotics.
- Those who spend time alone with the opposite sex.
- College students.
- Those who are dating.
- Those who are rich or want to be rich (1 Tim. 6:9–10).

To that list we could add all men (regarding pornography and sexual temptations or obsessive diversions) and all women (regarding pornography and sexual temptations or obsessive diversions). Temptations are common to us all. We should be concerned if we can't identify them; we are blessed if we can.

Our goal is to bring temptations out into the open and grow in saying no to restless desires (Titus 2:11–12). The apostle Paul puts it this way:

No temptation has overtaken you that is not common to man. God is faithful, and he will not let you be tempted beyond your ability, but with the temptation he will also provide the way of escape, that you may be able to endure it. (1 Cor. 10:13)

The story behind Paul's words is the time when Israel had left Egypt and was traveling through the wilderness. With hardships and dangers everywhere, they were more susceptible to temptations to trust other things. So we could add to our list of vulnerable people those who are going through chronic hardship.

So many behaviors that we call addictions start in the wilderness—times when life seems too hard. Life is difficult, and we prefer to avoid pain. God is not giving us the deliverance we want, so we look for relief in idols. We cut, drink, turn to porn, eat, smoke, snort, inject, take pills, play video games, read fantasy—all of these reveal our modern idols.

"What temptations are stalking you?"

"Could you pray for me on this next business trip? How about if I call you when I get to my room and we can pray for each other?"

"You have been in a hard place for a long time, and the longer it goes, the bigger the temptation to take matters into our own hands. With 1 Corinthians 10:13 in mind, how can I pray for those times when you face temptations?"

Those are the questions we will ask one another.

And if we think for a moment that God is asking us to be dour stoics who are banned from all fun, then we can be sure that we have lost a round or two in the spiritual battle. Keep in mind that all our help to one another should sound good. Our faith and obedience in temptation might be hard, but they bring maturity and satisfaction to life (James 1:2–4).

Our God "richly provides us with everything to enjoy" (1 Tim. 6:17). As such, saying no *protects* our capacity for enjoyment rather than diminishes it.

When We Have Seen Sin

The hardest sins to talk about are those we see someone commit, but we receive no invitation to speak. Here, we must decide if the sin is to be called out or covered.

Don't Be Silent Out of Fear

Most people who have witnessed sin or are even suspicious of it in another don't regret raising such important matters when they are raised well, but they do regret having been silent.

A church was left dazed when both a men's leader and a women's leader left their spouses, wrote a good-bye note to their families, and disappeared together. As a plan for pastoral care gradually developed, over a dozen people in the church said, "I should have said something." They had observed the way the two leaders had interacted and spoken about each other, and they regretted their silence.

When sin becomes public, especially when it is sin that damages relationships or incurs legal problems, so many think, "I should have said something." Yet we are slow to remember those mental notes. Our fear of people's angry reactions, the myth that help is needed only when asked for, and our sense that we have no right to say anything because we ourselves are quite a mess—these contribute to safe relationships rather than loving ones.

Don't Be Silent Out of Anger

If the sin has been against us, our anger is an even bigger problem than fear. The Old Testament puts it this way: "You shall not hate your brother in your heart, but you shall reason frankly with your neighbor, lest you incur sin because of him" (Lev. 19:17). When angry, we might be excellent at talking to others about someone's sin but wretched at talking to the actual sinner. Meanwhile, just a smidgeon of humility would remind us that we are rivaling the very sin we oppose as we stand in prideful judgment. If we are stuck in anger, *we* are the needy ones, and we ask for help.

Get Help

If we have any questions about how to proceed, we ask for help. We are part of a larger body, not private therapists, and we will often ask the larger body to help us to help others. And even when we ask for help, we proceed carefully. Confidences are important to us, and we want to speak well of people, so we might ask anonymously.

> "I think I should speak to someone about something I witnessed. Could you help me know what to say and even whether I should say it?"

A pastor would be an ideal person to ask.

Just the Facts

Our task is to hold up a mirror so that others see themselves more than they see us. We tell what we have actually seen; we avoid interpretations and usually stay away from speaking of how the actions might have hurt or disappointed us—that can wait for another time.

> "The other day I saw you walking down the street with Rich [not her husband]. Is everything okay? Should I be concerned?"

> "At the church meeting, you seemed pretty angry. I noticed that everyone went silent after you spoke, as if they were afraid to say anything. Could we talk about that?"

> "You seemed on edge this morning. When I asked about your upcoming day, you said my question was stupid. Is something wrong?"

> "I was thinking about our conversation the other day. When you talked about Jackie, you seemed to be holding some things against her. Could we talk about that?"

"When we were talking about your marriage, everything was about her—it was all her fault—and nothing was your own. I know things are complicated, but isn't our goal to be seeing our own faults long before we see our spouse's?"

Yes, any one of those comments would be difficult for most of us. But we are compelled by love. How would we want to be approached by someone who is aware of our public sin?

Be Prepared for Possible Negative Reactions

It doesn't always go well. The one we approach might get mad at us, which means we have probably identified something important. Anger is usually a self-indictment. Or the person becomes upset because we have been clumsy, self-righteous, or judgmental, in which case we are saddened, ask forgiveness, and grow in wisdom.

And what if the other does not accept our words and refuses to hear? Perhaps we wait, perhaps we persist because the matter is so important, perhaps we get advice from a wise friend, or perhaps we enlist someone else who has witnessed the sinful behavior and go together (Matt. 18:15–16). Love is what orients us. Fear or anger will blind us, but love and the best interests of others are our guide.

When Someone Discloses and Confesses Sin

When someone *discloses* sin, our help takes a different form, because the Spirit has already been on the move: the one sinning has taken his or her struggle public. The step from private to public is the biggest and hardest. Everything else is easy in comparison.

So when someone discloses sin, first, we see the good. Voluntary confession is evidence of spiritual power and deserves our admiration.

"Thank you so much for confessing this. I know there is more to be done, but no one can say what you said, apart from the Holy Spirit. This is real evidence that God is clutching on to you and won't let you go."

Don't Simply Commiserate

From there, a common mistake is either to match sin for sin or to sympathize in some way.

"I have struggled with porn too."

"She drives me crazy too."

Though our goal might be to make someone feel less alone or embarrassed by their confession, commiserating doesn't help. It shifts the conversation away from what is most important. Instead, we keep the focus on the issue at hand. We want to partner in an all-out battle against sin. The Spirit has started something, and we want to keep in step with what he is doing.

"What can I do to help?"

"What can *we* do to fight?"

"Let's develop a plan."

"Let's bring in some other people who can help."

To stay on track, offer partnership, humility, and patience but not commiseration.

Get to the Heart

Our understanding of sin is that it is a matter of the heart, which means that we are part of a process of redirecting the person's compass toward Jesus. Sin is about the Lord. It is personal and relational. God calls us friends, and when we sin, we temporarily abandon our connection to him. We prefer to manage aspects of our lives in our own way; we love our desires more than we love Jesus. At those times we need to be reminded of who God is and what he has done, who we are, and how we live in light of God's Word.

What God has done is this: with initiating love he has moved toward us. We simply respond to this love offensive—that is always the way of change. We call it "grace." That does not mean we are passive. It means that our lives are always responsive to God's first move toward us.

This strategy began with the Ten Commandments. The opening words are, "I am the Lord your God, who brought you out of the land of Egypt, out of the house of slavery" (Ex. 20:2). God identifies who he is—the gracious God who acts first.

Then he identifies who we are—a people once enslaved, now liberated, forgiven, and brought into the house of God.

Then he teaches us how to shape our lives according to the pattern of our Liberator.

The apostle Paul follows this same pattern. When you notice a "therefore" in his letters, it usually means that he has just told us about who Jesus is and what he has done, and he will now show us how to live for Jesus. What is important is that we begin with God.

So what has really been going on in the person's heart? Here are some clues:

"God cannot see me when I turn away from him."

"I have more freedom when I turn back to 'Egypt.'"

"I'm only human. Everyone sins. It's not treason, spiritual adultery, holding God in contempt, or dishonoring him."

"I have to be a better person now to get back into God's good graces."

"God is very upset rather than compassionate and merciful."

"I hadn't considered that I was bought with a great price and am no longer my own" (see 1 Cor. 6:20).

Each of those beliefs is an opportunity for confession and affirming the truth. If we feel less than competent at countering lies with truth, we get help from those who can, and we learn together.

Through it all we keep Jesus Christ in view. Here are just a few ways to do this:

- Read and talk about your favorite passage from Matthew, Mark, Luke, or John, or read through a New Testament book together.

- Have your friend read through her favorite passage about Jesus.

- Talk about the things of first importance—the death and resurrection of Jesus—and consider how that shapes the way we live.

Since you are engaged in a joint venture, everyone talks. Do you feel stuck? Pray together and enlarge the circle of those who help.

Develop a Plan

The knowledge of Jesus and our renewed allegiance to him lead to concrete action. We share our Internet sites with each other, we confess to those we sinned against, we consider amends where they might be appropriate, we walk away from a verbal fight rather than fuel it. There is something about the love of God that makes us very creative in generating concrete, small steps.

We stay away from vague, "I'm just going to try harder" kinds of commitments and instead have clear plans for how to do battle with Satan and sin and how to love others deeply from our hearts.

Is there a whiff of hopelessness? When hope fades, Satan is usually all over it. Time to get help.

If you are feeling overwhelmed, in over your head, get help. Why take on someone's burdens alone when a larger community is better equipped to carry the load?

Recognize the Messy Nature of Growth and Change

As we walk together, we observe, close up, the power of the Spirit. What could be better? The process, however, might be hard to see at first.

Spiritual growth follows the pattern we see all around us. Growth is barely perceptible from day to day. The baby has gained only an ounce or two, which is too little to be seen with the naked eye. The flower planted yesterday looks much the same today. And what if the baby gets sick or the flower is under-watered? For a moment, they might seem to be moving in the wrong direction. But week to week we can usually see something—an emerging double chin, a bulge on a stem that will become another flower.

In humans, this spiritual process is called "progressive sanctification." It means that growth and change are happening (Phil. 1:6) but not always as quickly as we would like.

So we keep our eyes peeled. If the person has the Spirit, we will see growth, though that growth is a spiritual battle.

Jim gave himself to alcohol for a decade. The reason he went to rehab and some AA meetings was that his wife was done threatening and was packing up to leave. In all that turmoil, he became a follower of Jesus. But he was confused. Nothing magical happened. He woke the next day with the same cravings and temptations. Where, he wondered, was the power of God?

A couple of wise friends noticed his despair. In response they were able to point out spiritual power in his life. Since he had changed spiritual allegiances, he had been crying out in prayer, and he had been doing that every day.

In other words, he was needy, which is a glorious step to being more fully human, as God intended. "Help" spoken to the Lord is power. The struggle itself is evidence of power; it means that he has been equipped to fight and is no longer a mere slave.

Mostly, spiritual power and growth feel like weakness, as if we just barely make it through the day.

Lead in Saying "Thank You" to God

As a hedge against hopelessness and despair, and as a way to affirm our dependence on the Lord, we lead the confessing one in saying "thank you."

"Thank you" means that we live because God graciously forgives our sins once and for all in Jesus. We are forgiven, not because we are so contrite and forgivable but because God's name is honored as he forgives us.

"Thank you" means that we are needy people, and, in forgiveness of sins and the Spirit's power, we have everything we need.

"Thank you" means that there is no long trip back to God after we come to our senses and turn from our sin. No, indeed.

Wherever we go, all we do is turn around, and our God is right there.

We have considered three occasions in which we will try to help people talk about sin:

- When someone faces temptations.
- When we have seen sin.
- When someone discloses and confesses sin.

Help will not be easy on these occasions, but it is help we can all give.

Discussion and Response

1) This is a long chapter. What stands out?
2) Do you believe you can do the things we've covered in this chapter? If so, have you actually done them? How did it go? If not, where do you need to grow?

We Are Needed

17

Keep *the* Story in View

Help can be so hard. Problems are complex. Relationships move forward in fits and starts. We try to avoid sounding trite, and we certainly don't want to say something wrong. It is easy to get lost in the course of helping one another.

In C. S. Lewis's *The Silver Chair*, Jill is sent off on a rousing and perilous task: "Seek this lost prince until either you have found him and brought him back to his father's house, or else died in the attempt, or else gone back to your own world."[9] Then she is given four signs that will keep her oriented through her journey. Without these she will be lost, so she is instructed to repeat them over and over to herself during her journey.

We need to do something similar on our journey. This is the way for both the helper and the person being helped to stay oriented: we remember *the* story.

The Bible's Master Story

You probably have a friend or family member who has told the same story dozens of times, but somehow, each time, you are still interested in hearing it. Stories that have this kind of staying power are not simply entertaining. They are instructive.

They are about the past but affect the present and might even point the way to a future.

That's what we want to do with Scripture. We want to be able to tell and retell the story and have it shape us. This will help us to remember it and quickly return to it when life's troubles come our way.

The apostle Paul always had this larger story in view. His mind was not an assortment of pithy sayings and pieces of advice. It was organized around Jesus Christ and the cosmic changes brought about by his life, crucifixion, and resurrection.

He told the larger story in different ways, and he wanted us to do the same thing—when you know a story well, you don't need a script and are always ready to add a new flourish here and there.

Ephesians 1:3–14 is a particularly rich way of telling it, and Paul's excitement is such that the original passage is one long, breathless sentence. The flow of his thought goes *from past, to present, to future*.

Read this psalm of praise as a way to get oriented to our spiritual reality. At least hold it in the background as the organizing story for your conversations.

This Is Your Past

Our past is a mess of good things and horrible things. The way we tell it at age twenty is different from the way we tell it at sixty. Paul assumes we all have our particular stories; he is telling the deeper one, one that we are all part of.

> He chose us in him before the foundation of the world, that we should be holy and blameless before him. In love he predestined us for adoption as sons through Jesus Christ. (vv. 4–5)

And what does this story of being chosen and predestined for adoption have to do with past victimization, rejection, or loss? It certainly does not minimize them. If anything, it shows their wrongness even more vividly because they are against God and his original intent. What the story does is counterbalance our past with a story of love, grace, and belonging that says, "Evil and misery will not win," and, "Things are not what they seem." Every retelling of the story, as it gathers more details of the blessings we have in Jesus, adds more weight to the master story.

This is reality for those who follow Jesus. This is what we see when we put on those glasses of faith. He pursued us. We were loved and adopted by him. This means that life in Christ is not an extended probation. Since his love is not dependent on our vacillating allegiances but on choices he made long ago, we rest in Jesus and have a revitalized purpose now that we are in the royal family.

This Is Your Present

God's persistent love through the ages moves to redemption and forgiveness of sins in the present. Everything hinges on this. If we are left in our sin, then we are separated from God. Only Christ's surprising sacrifice for us can bring the holy God so close that he never leaves.

> In him we have redemption through his blood, the forgiveness of our trespasses, according to the riches of his grace, which he lavished upon us, in all wisdom and insight making known to us the mystery of his will, according to his purpose. (vv. 7–9)

Why bother retelling that? Forgiveness of sins can seem a bit remote to people who either believe that their sins are not too big a deal or believe that forgiveness is too good to be true. Either way, Jesus is marginalized from daily life, and thankfulness is dependent on the events of the day rather than the unchanging blessings of God.

This part of the story sings when we remember that we are, indeed, sinners who turn away from God. Even when we care about others, we can never root out the selfishness, and, too often, obedience is merely a happy coincidence between what we want to do and what God says. So this deeper story works best when we are in the habit of confessing sins—"Forgive us our debts, as we also have forgiven our debtors" (Matt. 6:12).

Lavish grace. That is at the center of our present story.

This Is Your Future

A good story ends well. A story that ends badly renders everything else meaningless. Who cares about a good job today when death will eventually erode everything that came from it?

Hope is essential to human life. Without it we try to stay busy enough so that we are distracted by the bleak realities ahead. God's master story, of course, is the story of hope.

> [A plan has been set forth in Jesus Christ], a plan for the fullness of time, to unite all things in him, things in heaven and things on earth. In him you, when you believed in him, were sealed with the promised Holy Spirit, who is the guarantee of our inheritance until we acquire possession of it, to the praise of his glory. (assembled pieces of Eph. 1:9–14)

The part about "all things . . . in heaven and things on earth"? God's plans are to restore us—and creation itself. All things amiss now are to be gathered in under the activity of King Jesus. Everything will be made right. Something is afoot. Not only do we personally know forgiveness of sins; we are also brought into

God's plans to restore justice, beauty, reconciliation, and mercy. When we come to Jesus, life is suddenly jammed with purpose.

There are ways that we participate in those purposes even now. We have been brought into God's reclamation project, and simple acts of love, which echo God's justice, beauty, reconciliation, and mercy, are now incorporated into his kingdom plans. Everything done because of Jesus contributes to these final purposes. Death does not diminish them.

This hope strengthens us in the hardships and drudgeries of everyday life. Knowing where all things in heaven and earth are headed, we can wait and persevere (1 Thess. 1:2), and that endurance or perseverance is key to a life well lived. Without it we are left with grumbling, addiction, or despair. With it, we look ahead and tell a different story than the present distress tries to tell. Whereas chronic suffering assumes that nothing will ever change, hope knows that our rescuer is committed to our good. Hope knows the love of Jesus and grows in confidence that all the promises God makes have already been *yes* in Jesus.

As Paul tells the story, the Lord's generosity and faithfulness began before recorded time and extend forever. He is certain of that. Our inheritance in Jesus is assured, because the Spirit himself holds it for us.

Perhaps we will start considering new questions and have different conversations.

"Do you ever think about when heaven will come to earth? What do you think it will be like?"

"Do you ever wonder what it will be like to be without sin?"

And such conversations are actually a way we grow in Christ. For example, when we have the hope of seeing Jesus face-to-face, and we know that hope is certain, our lives become organized around that meeting. When we look forward to sinless perfection, we are inspired to grow today into who we will be.

How can we make the master story fresh on every retelling, whether we tell it all or only mention one episode? Children are naturals with stories. They want to hear the same story over and over, and each time the story draws them in. They are not just watching a bear hunt—they are *on* the bear hunt; they are twirling in front of a rapt audience; they are riding the horse no one thought could be tamed. They are our models for keeping the master story in view, which again reminds us that this task of helping one another is for all ordinary people.

Discussion and Response

1) How would you retell the master story? Do you have a favorite part?
2) How does retelling the story change your everyday life?

Conclusion

A Community Works Best Side by Side

A man was sitting across the table from his friend, talking about important matters—a recent confession of daily pornography, a hard marriage, financial problems. As they were slogging through this debris, the man sensed that something was askew. He didn't like the way that he and his friend were sitting. So he got up and moved his chair so that he was *next to* rather than across from his friend, and—everything changed. Information became much more personal, tears flowed, prayer was natural. Side by side is most suitable for helping. We nudge the person beside us with affection; we hold hands; we put our hand on a shoulder; we put our arm around the one next to us.

We notice the same positioning in Jesus's life on earth. He was the teacher—of that there is no doubt—but he is Immanuel, God with us, so he was always eating a meal with people, sitting side by side. This was his way of saying to the invitees, "You are my people. I identify with you; you can identify with me."

You Are Needy and You Are Needed

Keep that dinner table in view. It is a larger group. Better yet, picture a community—a church—being side by side with us as we know and help others. We started all this by recounting how we need one another's help when we have troubles. That neediness now extends to how we need one another's help *when we help*. Since we do not have all human gifts, abilities, and experience in ourselves, we usually need cohelpers.

A young woman confides in you that she is cutting herself as a way to deal with life. Even though she has been cutting for over a year, you can't be certain about the dangers, so you let her know that the two of you will enlarge the number of people who know. Her mother will be one, and you will add people from there—perhaps her small-group leader, her pastor, a medical doctor, and someone familiar with cutting. When there is possible physical danger, helpers always get help.

> For as in one body we have many members, and the members do not all have the same function, so we, though many, are one body in Christ, and individually members one of another. Having gifts that differ according to the grace given to us, let us use them. (Rom. 12:4–6)

Problems *are* complex. Even relatively simple matters, such as child discipline, can be complex. As a counselor, I am always getting help from other pastors and counselors; and helping someone in the context of a group, in which all of us will pray for and help the one in need, is ideal.

The basic platform for help that we have just reviewed is good and helpful in all hardships. In fact, it is *necessary* for all of us in our suffering and sin. It is necessary, but, in many situations, we help as part of a larger community.

Humility and patience—they will serve us well as we serve others. They take the fear out of helping as we remember that "the body does not consist of one member but of many" (1 Cor. 12:14).

For by the grace given to me I say to everyone among you not to think of himself more highly than he ought to think, but to think with sober judgment, each according to the measure of faith that God has assigned. (Rom. 12:3)

And all these gifts exist so we can serve one another in love.

Notes

1. Luke 6:43–45 echoes all of these analogies.
2. Scripture poses different questions of the heart. They all concern our divine allegiances. Who do you love? (Deut. 6:5; 1 John 2:15); who do you trust? (Jer. 17:5–8); who (or what) do you worship? (2 Kings 17:36); who will you serve? (Matt. 6:24); who do you obey? (1 John 3:10); for whose glory do you live? (Rom. 1:21–23); where is your treasure—is it in the world or in Christ? (Matt. 6:21); to whom do you belong? (John 8:44). To these we can add other questions. What do you crave? What do you feel that you need? Where do you find refuge, comfort, pleasure, or security? Who are your heroes and role models? What defines success or failure for you? When do you say, "If only . . . ?" (e.g., "If only my husband would . . .") What do you see as your rights? Where in your life have you struggled with bitterness? What or whom do you avoid? Do you feel guilty at times?
3. R. Weiss and S. Mirin, *Cocaine* (Washington, DC: American Psychiatric Association, 1987), 55.
4. Eugene Heimler, *Concentration Camp* (New York: Pyramid, 1959), 31–32.
5. C. S. Lewis, *The Horse and His Boy* (New York: Harper Trophy, 1954), 174.
6. Similar psalms include 23; 40; 42; 46; 51; 62; 63; 73; 77; 84; 116; 121; 131.
7. God is the host who invites us to the banquet (Isa. 55:1–3). He is the Father who knows us by name (Isa. 45:3). He is the king who calls us friends and says that we should call him by his very personal names. Among the worst sins is betrayal that says, "I do not know the man" (Matt. 26:74). Among the great blessings is to know and be known.
8. Dietrich Bonhoeffer, *Life Together* (San Francisco: Harper & Row, 1954), 112.
9. C. S. Lewis, *The Silver Chair* (New York: Harper Trophy, 1953), 23.

General Index

General Index

Scripture Index

Download a free study guide at
crossway.org/SidebySide

CCEF

Restoring Christ to Counseling and Counseling to the Church

COUNSELING
ccef.org/counseling

WRITING
ccef.org/resources

TEACHING
ccef.org/courses

EVENTS
ccef.org/events

"CCEF is all about giving hope and help with a 'heart.' If you want to learn how to effectively use God's Word in counseling, this is your resource!"

Joni Eareckson Tada, Founder and CEO, Joni and Friends International Disability Center

Christian Counseling & Educational Foundation
ccef.org